CORRUPTION

A Perspective to Its Understanding and Eradication

OLUSEGUN ODETOYINBO

authorHOUSE®

AuthorHouse™ UK
1663 Liberty Drive
Bloomington, IN 47403 USA
www.authorhouse.co.uk
Phone: 0800.197.4150

Published by AuthorHouse 04/29/2019

ISBN: 978-1-5462-9673-7 (sc)
ISBN: 978-1-5462-9674-4 (hc)
ISBN: 978-1-5462-9672-0 (e)

Contents

I dedicate this book to my children and grandchildren for their love and support, and to all those people who have had an impact on my life, work, and health.

Preface

There are many scholarly publications about corruption and its effects. Some of these are specific to certain areas of the world, while others are general and apply to all areas. In some parts of the world, corruption has become a way of life; in other countries, it is subtle and may not directly affect people's way of life because there are processes in place against it. Also, there is efficiency and accountability in those societies. A corrupt government is unlikely to initiate anticorruption measures and vigorously pursue them. The population needs to be informed, educated, and offered suggestions to empower the individual to get involved in the processes that help to eradicate corruption in their societies. Building the knowledge and skills to combat corruption helps individuals make good choices in electing good leaders into political office.

This book is a short piece that looks at corruption, its causes and effects, and offers some understanding of the issue of corruption. The answers and suggestions are not very comprehensive, but I hope it will stimulate some thinking and get people to make a change. Change must be voluntary by all individuals, who must understand the reason for the change and be committed to effecting the change. The general population needs to be involved and have a say in issues that affect them, from the local level up to the national level. Cultural and other issues need to be seen in context and addressed. As they say, you cannot get something new if you keep doing the same things the same old way.

OO

1

Corruption: An Overview and a Case for Change

***Corruption (definition):** Bribery, extortion, fraud, cartels, abuse of power, embezzlement, money-laundering and other similar activities.*

The definition of these criminal practices, examples of each, why they occur, and how they occur is well detailed by various publications and research studies. International anticorruption organisations are also good sources.

This practice is present to some extent and in various severities in all societies. Corruption usually occurs because some individuals are willing to use illicit means to maximise personal or corporate profit. However, for these individuals to become involved in corrupt activity, circumstances must exist which do not prevent or discourage them from doing so.

Everybody talks about it, we see it in action, and we feel its effects personally, on relatives, and in the community. We report it and write brilliant pieces on it in the local and social media, and we pray and cast out the corruption demon. It has become a way of life in some countries and is 'unconsciously' accepted even though the corrupt are a small minority. It has become a circle (and a never-ending one) because everybody falls in and it rolls along. It is fuelled by ignorance, lack of education, greed, selfishness, lack of love and compassion for fellow human beings, and indifference.

The cycle has to be broken and the nation sorted out permanently. This process is not a quick-fix process. Even if we put into power a brutal dictator-like regime that imprisons corrupt people and seizes their assets and forces people to fall in line, the suppressed corrupt will plot to get rid of the regime, and the seed of corruption will sprout again (sound familiar?). The seeds of honesty must be sown and be watered by education, compassion, hard work, and a community orientation that respects contributions to society, not what can be stolen from it. The motto for aspiring politicians and political parties is 'You are in it to serve and not to be rich.' Change must start from all levels of the society; it must be conscious, directed, coordinated, and managed. It will not start or change by chance. The corrupt government cannot start this process. There is a need for a nongovernment funded organisation against corruption. The elimination of corruption is a very deliberate goal. It should, therefore, be declared not only in the government's statement of policy but in particular a 'government anti-corruption strategy' document, a binding list of changes that must be made within the framework of the fight against corruption, including stipulated deadlines. Also, its fulfilment will be regularly and thoroughly monitored. All members must be geared toward eradicating corruption. *Eradication of corruption starts with you.*

The first step in making a change is to recognise that there is something wrong or that there is a new goal or target to meet. Change will not come on its own; it needs a direct and conscious effort on the part of the individual or group that requires the change.

Eradication of corruption starts with you. Yes, *you*. Those who are corrupt do not know any better; they are not honest, they are lazy, and they are unwilling to work hard and do not want change. Some of those who know that corruption is destroying society and still join in just moan and display ambivalence.

Make a conscious effort to change the status quo in your own way. You must be anticorruption in all your walks of life, starting in the home. Teach your children (with your own actions) to be honest and that hard work has its reward and is good for self-worth, that nothing comes out of nothing, that there is no shortcut to life and achievement. Teach them that the path through life is not plain sailing and is full of ups and down and that life's events are seasonal. Teach love, compassion, and respect for their fellow human beings. Teach them respect for the laws of the country.

Schools. The same values should be taught to every child at the primary and secondary level. In addition to this is a sense of national pride—basic civics, the responsibilities of each person as members of the community, respect of fellow citizens and their views and for those in authority. Teach the importance of accountability in personal and in public office.

At work and every day. Each citizen should determine to practise anticorruption and expose corruption in their daily lives. Do your work diligently and honestly, according to your job description. Expose corruption in your workplace. Discuss unusual and unacceptable work practices. Organisations, in addition to vetting their employees on being employed, need to train them about corruption in the workplace and how to deal with bribes or other forms of corruption, if encountered. Cooperate with law-enforcement agencies and the media to expose corruption. Work ethic should be developed in the society. There should be a charter for top officials and a means of monitoring them. There should be transparency and public openness to government activities. A code of practice should be in place. Ongoing evaluation and assessment and appraisal processes should be in place. There should be good governance in place in government and in all public institutions.

Contracts. The power of an individual in office to award a multi-billion-dollar contract is a recipe for corruption. There should be a transparent and publicised contract-award process, conducted by a panel. There should be standardised costing to bring down excessive inflation of contracts. Allow only transparent companies to bid for contracts. The declaration of interest must be made by everyone connected with the contract award.

All organisations should implement a management programme to prevent, detect, and deal with corruption both within their own organisation and in their dealings with their business associates. An anticorruption programme and template, as well as further resources suitable for any organisation, in any country, are available on the GIACC

(Global Infrastructure Anti-Corruption Centre) website (http://www. giaccentre.org/project_companies.php).

Each government office, public institution, and company must have a work charter. The charter tells what the institution is about, how it meets your needs, how it does it, and within which period. The charter must contain an anticorruption statement and programme to prevent, detect, and deal with corruption. It must outline what to do if you are not happy with their services. You, the public, can rate them and their services by self- or externally-conducted surveys.

The press and media. The press and media have a duty to expose corruption, not only reporting it but actively doing investigative journalism. The press must be independent and not politically influenced. It has a duty to inform the nation and to champion people's rights, to expose incompetence and corruption in high offices.

Law-enforcement agents. In a corrupt society, the police are usually corrupt and the institutions meant to be independent are controlled by corrupt politicians. Crime and corruption will breed when people know they will not be caught because the police are incompetent and can be bribed. There needs to be an overhaul of the police from the top (retire corrupt officers), as well as higher recruitment standard, training, and equipment. A sense of professionalism and accountability should be fostered in the police. The first step is not to offer bribes to the police but to educate the public about the role and standards expected of the police. Everybody should not give bribes and demand their rights.

The judiciary. The corrupt members need to be exposed and removed. A robust system for appointment and appraisal of its members should be in place.

Politicians/leadership. Strong leadership that has a vision for any nation is required. Leaders need likeminded people around them. Change is needed from above. The electorate has to be aware of what it wants and to elect the right people, who are accountable to the people.

> *A people that elect corrupt politicians, impostors, thieves, and traitors are not victims but accomplices.*
>
> —George Orwell

Imagine you are employing a person. At the interview, he promises to do his job, and occupants of a high office may even influence you by bringing gifts (or what politicians do in their constituencies leading up to elections). After you have employed him, your money and valuables are progressively stolen, and he becomes a lord unto himself and does not do the job he is expected to do. In real life, you or a company will sack the individuals or persecute them. If they apply for the job again, they will never be short-listed or reemployed. The nation keeps reemploying (voting) these same corrupt people or political parties.

The standard of honesty, decency, commitment, and work ethic which is required of politicians is very high. They must make rules and manage the affairs and finances of the state, fairly and without partiality and having the state's interest at heart. High office commands respect, and the occupant of the office must behave in a manner that befits the office and not in a way that disrespects the office and the people.

Educate the People

People must be educated about politicians to know that

- They go into politics to serve, not to get rich and not to steal.
- They do their jobs. They are accountable to you. They must be made to resign if they are not doing their jobs or are fraudulent.
- They should have a vision; they are willing to serve and have the experience.
- Politicians are not above the laws of the country.

Effects of Corruption

Corruption is considered to be one of the main obstacles to the development of democracy. It undermines democratic values and good governance and negatively affects the formal democratic processes.

Public institutions and government departments which are mainly created for the delivery of public services are the units of the democratic system. When the officials of these institutions engage in corrupt activities, the institutions lose their credibility.

Corrupt societies lack sound political competition. The decisions are often made based on personal authority rather than legal authority, which in turn undermine democratic values. These issues finally lead to anger and frustration in the citizens. Corrupt elections have reduced the amount of accountability and responsiveness in the elected official to the public. In the judiciary, corruption compromises the rule of law and responsibility to the public. More generally, corruption has decreased the capacity of governmental institutions. Many procedures in government institutions are considered useless. The public wealth and public resources are unequally distributed; high offices are often bought and sold. Corruption has also undermined the legitimacy of the government and has negatively affected public trust and tolerance.

Economy. Corruption causes the misuse of national wealth by a small group of the population. It often results in the unequal distribution of wealth, and it increases the cost of goods and the delivery of public service by the following means: (i) prevention of economic growth; (ii) reduction in the effectiveness of international assistance; and (iii) loss of tax revenue, as bribes are paid to evade taxes and customs. In corrupt societies, corruption causes the transformation of public wealth into private wealth and neglects the necessities of the public. The funds are spent on unnecessary projects, and the basic needs of citizens are ignored.

Society. Socially, corruption discourages people from working together for the common good of society. It disturbs social services delivery and increases frustration among citizens, which results in a weak civil society. Corruption increases poverty in society and increases the gap between the rich and poor. In a corrupt society, paying and taking bribes becomes a tradition which results in inequality, hatred, and insecurity. According to a UNDP publication, 'Corruption: A Primer—December 2008', corruption increases the price of public services and lowers their quality' Furthermore, paying bribes for public service frustrate citizens and demoralises citizen's trust on the government which causes social unrest.

Everybody understands that corruption will not do any good to anyone. It harms everybody and society. So, in order to get rid of this serious issue and live in a corruption-free society, everybody should take a stand against corruption. Both government and citizens have to take a stand and make the fight against corruption one of the top priorities for the development and stabilisation of their beloved country.

2

How Corruption Affects People and Communities

Corruption has a devastating effect on the communities in which it occurs especially if it has become a way of life. It threatens

- Sustainable economic development
- Ethical values and justice
- Rule of law

It destabilises society. It delays infrastructure development and facilitates poor building quality and layers additional cost.

People. Corruption has many negative effects on people:

- There is no quality of service. You have to pay for it. Services and infrastructure are unequally distributed. Government institutions are corrupt and less effective. People have to bribe for services to ensure they are provided timely and efficiently.
- There is no job satisfaction. People with no ability or qualification get into posts. This affects the efficiency and performance of an institution.
- There is injustice due to corruption in the judiciary. Victims of offence suffer as they are not assured justice.

- Police incompetence and corruption delays crime investigation. It allows the breakdown of the rule of law and increased crime rate. Criminals roam free and may even commit further crimes.
- It creates unemployment. The economy is poor. There is a decrease in foreign investment and job creation. The infrastructure (electricity, road and rail network, water supply) needed for industry are non-existent or non-functioning due to misappropriation of or lack of funds for their construction, or due to corruption. The country depends on imports, and there are no manufacturing industries to generate income for the country. The cost of running a business is increased, leading to higher cost to consumers.
- There is increased cost of living and increase incidence of poverty. This results from a combination of poor economy, unemployment, poor pay, and the exorbitant cost of living.
- People's health issues are affected due to absence of clean water, poor environmental sanitation, increased pollution, poor quality of food, and lack of medication. There is a lack of facilities in hospitals. A healthy nation is a wealthy one.
- Poor roads make transportation difficult and lead to road accidents. Others include vehicle licensing and poor vehicle roadworthiness, inadequate servicing due to costs/corruption. Driving licences are issued to people who have not satisfied driving licensing requirements/tests. Lack of enforcement of road regulations also leads to increased road traffic accident rates.
- There is lack of faith in the government to provide services, especially in a government with no good governance processes.
- Lack of investment in education due to the allocated funds having been misappropriated. Corruption in the admission systems to institutions. Donations to prestigious universities to enable donors' children admission. Poor quality of education due to lack of facilities or corruption of the awards by the universities.
- Aversion to joining posts linked to corruption. This deters bright people from going into politics, joining the police force, etc.

Corruption and Human Psychology

Many wonder why people in corrupt societies do not stand up against the system. There are various factors, according to psychological studies. Some of these are **social pressure**, **dependency**, and **fear**.

Social pressure. The need to have money and fulfil social obligations causes a majority to participate in corruption, offering or accepting bribes. People have no social responsibility to do anything about it and lapse into a state of **dependency** on the system, and this gives an excuse for participation in and justification of the system. There is a sense of lack of control, and the greater this loss of control, the more people adapt to the corrupt system and justify and defend it.

Fear. People feel threatened by the politicians and corrupt leaders, who in some cases have uncontrolled power. People fear lack of justice if the system is opposed and they get arrested.

3

Effects of Corruption on a Country

Corruption affects all aspects of the community and the country as a whole. It breaks up systems that are in place, and it is rife where there are no systems in place. It becomes a way of life; even though people complain about it, they have to live with it. They expect a change from the government which is corrupt and which prefers the status quo to a change. Individuals cautiously write and talk about corruption but rarely organise a group to fight corruption. Individuals do not want to put their lives and those of their relatives at risk from the corrupt, who will do anything to continue in power. The justice system is often also corrupted, and nobody will sacrifice themselves without an assurance that justice will be done.

Unity. The fight against corruption starts with everybody as individuals. In a corrupt country, every citizen, irrespective of their racial, tribal, or religious origin, have a lot in common. A country should be united and focus on its commonalities and resolve to do something about what they are not happy about.

They all live within the same boundary, called their country and should focus on the present and not what they believe about the creation of the country. Politicians are expected to preserve national unity and govern by passing legislation and making decisions that are not partial but designed for the good of the country as a whole.

You share a common history. Learn from the lessons of history and stop pointing fingers and stirring strife and disunity by playing the blame game.

Your children and your future generations are going to continue living in the country. Aim to leave them a better and more prosperous country than the present corrupt one. You are all affected by the evils of corruption. You share the same infrastructure and economy that has been and is still being destroyed by corruption. You have local and national governments (elected by you) who are ineffective due to internal corruption among politicians. Corrupt politicians are not in power to serve and improve the country and the lives of all citizens. These politicians are not likely to wake up and start a true anticorruption programme. It has to start with you, the citizen.

Let us look at some features that affect us and which we want to change and improve.

Bread. I use this to signify the need for a country to be able to feed itself, have food in abundance, and export surpluses to earn money for the country. A country that depends on imports to feed itself is at the mercy of those who grow the food and has the risk of high food prices, with serious consequences for the low-income groups in the community. Get the government to grow more food by investing in agricultural projects.

Education. This is a key factor in the development of the country and is a tool for fighting corruption. Education leads to empowerment. There should be no obstacle to having a basic education. Education must have relevant content, have high quality and standards, and be useful at all levels. It should build in the student personal development, decision making, national pride, and respect for fellow citizens. This should be delivered by highly prized, knowledgeable, and skilled teachers.

A good quality education has been described as 'one that provides all learners with capabilities they require to become economically productive, develop sustainable, livelihoods, contribute to peaceful and democratic societies and enhance individual wellbeing' (VVOB).

The quality of education cannot be guaranteed in a corrupt country. Educational funding is low or misappropriated, causing lack of adequate facilities (building, textbooks, and equipment) in schools and universities. There is often no equity in access to education. Admission criteria are often corrupted.

Training of teachers must be of high professional quality, with only the best ones employed in schools and higher institutions. Recruitment, promotion, and appointment of teachers are all subject to corruption. If examinations and assessments of students are corrupted, the education standards fall.

Economy. This simply means the wealth of the country, the state of the country regarding the production and consumption of goods and services and the supply of money. It is evident in a corrupt society that there is no careful management of the available resources. The politicians entrusted with this important aspect of the country have not done any jobs at all. Money generated is not spent for the benefit of the country but are stolen by individuals and deposited outside the country. Are revenue and job-creating projects being carried out at all levels of government (local and national)?

Foreign investors will not be comfortable investing in a corrupt country with no reliable infrastructure. No wealth is created in the country, and no new jobs are created. Unemployment rate rises.

Infrastructure. These are fundamental facilities and systems serving a country, including services and facilities necessary for its economy to function. These include roads, bridges, railways, power supply, gas and electricity, and water resources. These are not luxuries but basic, a must for a country to function and develop its economy. Effective infrastructure attracts investments and investors, hence economic development and job creation and employment of citizens. Manufacturing industries and exports create wealth for the country and improve the economy.

National identity. Citizens must have a sense of national identity, service, and pride. This must be incorporated into the education system at all levels. We have a lot in common as a country and should not fractionate along tribal, regional levels. It starts in the home. Teach your children to

- Be country conscious, not feed them old stories of intertribal hatred and distrust.
- Respect and have consideration for their fellow countrymen irrespective of gender, religion, or ethnicity. Treat fellow men with care and compassion.
- Be good citizens. Respect and obey the laws of the country and demand justice and equality for all.

The government should provide an effective law and justice system to facilitate law and order, equality, and justice in the country. National identity fragments in a corrupt society. When legislation, distribution of funds, and key appointments favour a tribal, ethnic, or religious group, other sections of the country feel marginalised.

Governance. The manner of governing the country needs to change. The concept of hard work, service, and orderliness in all things should be taught in the educational system (and homes). Leadership means service, humility, and high standards of effectiveness and carries with it accountability to the people. Processes must be in place that allow smooth running of institutions and which put in checks to ensure accountability, transparency, and honesty in public life. When these are not in place or disregarded due to corruption, the government cannot run efficiently.

Morale. The confidence, attitude, enthusiasm, self-esteem, and discipline of a country's population are down when corruption is rife. When there is low morale, there is no feeling of satisfaction. This affects productivity in government, business, and all aspects of life. Among the things that affect people's morale are poor rewards for effort or jobs, especially when salaries are not paid on time or are insufficient to sustain families for another month. Lack of motivation and dedication result from the effects of corruption on the society. Other factors include unemployment, lack of basic infrastructure, poor sanitation and health facilities, and lack of adequate law enforcement and justice system.

4

Psychology and Cultural Aspects of Corruption

What makes a person become corrupt? This is multifactorial.

a. **Personality traits**. This includes people who have the traits mentioned below, who are more prone to corruption:

- **Impaired empathy**. These individuals struggle to put themselves in the shoes of another or understand how their actions may affect the wellbeing of someone else.
- **Self-centeredness**. Individuals who prioritise their own needs over those of others.
- **Manipulation**. Individuals who deceptively influence systems or other people's perceptions.
- **Entitlement**. These individuals believe that they deserve to succeed or have their needs met more than others and that they deserve special treatment. This affects their behaviour in life and in office.
- **Tendency to project blame on to others**. These individuals avoid taking responsibility for their own actions.

Other characteristics associated with corruption include thrill-seeking behaviour, social conformity, the need for instant gratification, risk-taking behaviour, a strong need for power, and possession of a 'poverty spirit', i.e., the constant need to accumulate wealth.

b. **Greed**. Human beings are innately greedy. Some people can contain the urge for self-enrichment and instant gratification; others cannot. When it comes to corrupt public officials, if there is a prospect for self-gratification, they are likely to grab it with both hands unless they are monitored closely. If there is a lack of monitoring and accountability in governments, this opens up the potential for corruption. Corruption is often committed to supplement an inadequate income, especially among lower paid public servants. The dichotomy is money-for-greed versus money-for-need.

c. **Culture**. Individuals with corruption bound together. An isolated corrupt person cannot survive. There is the notion of the cultural concept of sharing. Cultural values, such as the 'need for sharing and caring', may lead to pressure to behave corruptly. 'The propensity of corruption may lie in the need of certain people to share and care (or perhaps more accurately, to be seen to share and care), as much as it may be traced to greed, a sense of entitlement and the need to be seen as successful' (Moerdyk 2013).

d. **Parental influence/early upbringing**. An individual's morality and ethics are based on the process of socialisation as well as on modelling and education from parents or caregivers. We learn behaviour from our parents and teachers. The family provides a framework for the development of an individual. According to psychologists, 'The Family provides a framework within which human beings may find roots, continuity and a sense of belonging. Parents serve as the first socialising agents. Especially, sound family environment always presents disciplines, moral and obedience lessons. Mainly, such diversified effective lessons impart good manners, corruption free minds, and an acquired integrated personality' (Upadhyay 2003). Psychologists also agree that a person's moral and ethical development can be disturbed by dire social and economic circumstances in which personal survival is prioritised above everything else.

18

e. **Attitudes of society and the public**. Corruption will not thrive in a society whose moral, social, and economic situation does not permit it. When corruption has been operating in a country over many years, it becomes self-perpetuating and destroys the economy and moral well-being of the society. It becomes a monumental problem that needs to be tackled.

The Influence of a Country's Culture on Corruption

Culture can be defined as the collectively shared beliefs about right and wrong and what is permitted and what is not. Corruption is not purely a case of rotten apples. Rather, the barrel or orchard is contaminated. Corruption can be ingrained in an environment so that everyone is infected. The organisational culture influences the extent of corruption among employees who are operating it. Cultural expectations may predispose individuals to corruption, especially if the individual cannot rise above it. Some cultures expect that the appointment of a person from their region or tribe will mean diversion of funds and award of contracts to develop the area, to the detriment of other parts of the country. The individual is now expected to behave in a defined fashion or status which is financially above their new status. These may predispose the individual to corrupt practices if there are no tight checks and processes in place. This is a conception based on the false notion that politicians in office are rich and the wealth must flow down. Education of the people is required to counter these old views.

Corruption is not a cultural issue; all countries and cultures value honesty and integrity and will not condone the use of public funds for personal use. There are, however, cultural values and practices that may predispose one to corruption.

Giving vs Bribery

Alwyn Moerdyk, a lecturer in organisational psychology at Rhodes University, says that culture is often used to explain or excuse acts of corruption. Some societies claim that gift-giving is 'part of our culture' and outsiders should not confuse it with bribery. Moerdyk notes that the act of giving is a natural process for humans and is an expression of gratitude for a benefit received or to cement a relationship. But the size of the gift, or the context in which it was given, may make that gift a bribe. Gifts have the purpose of cementing existing relationships, whereas bribes are designed to create new relationships. A past president of Nigeria makes a distinction between gifts and bribes. In the African concept of appreciation and hospitality, he explains, the gift is usually a token. It is not demanded. The value is usually in the spirit rather than in the material worth. It is usually done in the open and never in secret. Where it is excessive, it becomes an embarrassment, and it is returned.

Companies and government offices should actively dissuade gift-giving before services are provided. There should be a gift policy document which should be widely available to the public and displayed in institutions. The policy should not be ambiguous; it should advise workers to report gifts, which should be returned if it can be deemed a bribe. It should also define what company hospitality gifts to receive and give out. The relevant taxation implications should be included in the policy.

Rule vs Leadership

Traditionally elders are respected and generally deemed to be wise. Hence they are in the council of elders who administer the villages. They say what need to be done. This rolled on to the colonial era, when the colonial masters tell administrators what to do. By and large, early politicians took the leadership role in getting independence. Subsequent politicians and people in authority have reverted to rulership and telling what to do instead of a fully democratic involvement of the population. As a result of corruption this system has developed into a situation where in some countries older people are in power. They form a cartel who decide who is appointed to prominent posts for which they are not qualified. They even control the candidates who run for election in the parties instead of allowing party members to do this. Younger party members cannot make changes and have to form an alliance with prominent party politicians. When elected, these younger politicians are still influenced by the 'godfathers' or 'kingmakers'. Politicians give money to respected and influential people in the society, e.g., traditional rulers and religious leaders who tell their followers for whom to vote. Frequently these kingmakers disagree or fall out, there is no communication, and the issue becomes a personal battle rather than a democratic decision process for the good of the nation. Hence, younger able and qualified people are unwilling to be involved in politics and its corrupt and dirty antics.

Scholars refer to this as *power distance*. Power distance is defined as the degree to which members of a society distribute, deploy, and react to the application of power, authority, and status. Power distance reflects the relationship between those who have the power and those who do not. Countries that are high in power distance tend to expect obedience toward superiors and clearly distinguish between those with status and power and those without. These societies are likely to be more corrupt than those that have a low power distance.

Assertiveness and Corruption

Assertiveness refers to the extent to which a society encourages people to be tough, confrontational, assertive, and competitive versus modest and tender. Such characteristics will encourage people to fight unethical values and practices. Therefore, societies with a high level of assertiveness are expected to have a lower level of corruption. The higher the level of assertiveness values and practices, the lower the level of corruption.

Gender Egalitarianism and Corruption

Gender egalitarianism refers to societies that seek to minimise differences between the roles of females and males in homes, organisations, and communities (Emrich et al. 2004). Some societies with high levels of gender egalitarianism seek to minimise gender differences and encourage women to participate equally in society. There are more educated women and women in position of authority. Research shows that there is a low level of corruption where more women are in parliament and that the level of corruption is less when women head organisations. Women are more social oriented, while men are individually oriented (selfish). When faced with economic decisions, women are more generous and exhibit helping behaviour. Societies with high gender egalitarianism tend to be less corrupt.

Individual Collectivism and Corruption

Individual collectivism refers to the strength of ties within small groups, such as family and close friends. In such countries, family members and close friends have strong expectations from each other. People can break the rules and regulations to meet those expectations. In collectivist cultures, networks of friends and families are more oriented towards creating strong relationships that facilitate illegal transactions. Therefore, family connections might encourage corruption.

In societies that score high on individualism,

- It is very common to favour a close friend or family member in recruiting or in allocating rewards and promotions.
- Individual goals take precedence over group goals, people emphasise rationality, and individuals are likely to engage in activities alone.
- Individual tend to apply different standards, laws, regulations, and explanations to different groups and situations.

Double standards exist in a collectivist society. The level of corruption is expected to increase. The higher the level of individual collectivism values and practices, the higher the level of corruption.

Effects of Religion

There are many scholarly articles and work on religion and corruption. What are the effects of religion on corruption? Has religion become corrupt, thereby losing its moral influence? Most religions do not condone corruption but advocate good behaviour, morals, and living in harmony in society. Does religion have an effect on the morality and acceptable behaviour of the society? To what extent does each of the major religions actively engage their followers in the practical application of their teaching in the daily challenges they face in society? Religion is one of the many factors that form the attitudes towards moral issues. Other issues include age, education level, gender, engagement with a wider community, the nature of the religious community(ies) involved, the nature of the moral issue itself, and so on. Religion itself, in terms of theological teaching, appears to have little influence on attitudes towards moral issues related to corruption. Socialisation is a much more important factor. The individual's religion may not be the only factor that personally influences their attitude or justification of corrupt behaviour.

Religious traditions have often been thought to condition cultural attitudes towards social hierarchy. Where more 'hierarchical religions'— Catholicism, Eastern Orthodoxy, Islam—dominate, challenges to officeholders might be rarer than in cultures shaped by more egalitarian or individualistic religions, such as Protestantism.

Corruption within the church/religious organisation appears less frequently in the formal religions with a structure and in which there is a central control or accountability of priests and branches of the religion.

Independent religious bodies—self-established, managed by individuals—are subject to the individual leader's religious and personal goals. What sets out with a pure intention is more likely to lose focus due to interaction with the norms of the society and the financial issues involved with running of the organisation. Sources of funding and donation are not scrutinised but may be accepted even if the source is corrupt.

The separation between the state and religion may allow the Church to play a role in monitoring and denouncing abuses by state officials. In other traditions—such as Islam—where religion and state hierarchies are closely intertwined, such a role may be absent.

In multi-religious societies, it is best that the state involvement in religion is minimal save when it involves the law and order and safeguarding rights of individuals or communities. The government should not be partial.

In countries which are traditionally affiliated to one religion, the rights of other religion to exist and for individuals to practice their religion should be respected. Corruption should be tackled as a separate issue, with or without religious input.

Religions may also influence how individuals view their loyalties to the family as opposed to other citizens—what Edward Banfield has called 'familism'—which, in turn, may affect the level of nepotism.

Does religion affect the quality of government, making it less corrupt? Theoretically, it should, if a majority of legislators abide by the good teaching of their religion and possess the right qualities. Legislators are individuals and are subject to the same factors that makes a person chose to be corrupt. Clean legislators cannot make impact where the majority are corrupt. It is therefore essential to scrutinise candidates and politicians and to vote in the right people.

5

Psycho-Sociology of Corruption

To effectively combat corruption we need to pay more attention to the individual social psychology of corrupt behaviour. There is a need to understand why a person might act dishonestly and in particular to consider how an individual's tendency to commit corrupt acts may depend on both the person's moral identity and the surrounding circumstances. Organisations are also affected by psycho-sociological factors, which determine its organisational cultures.

What motivates individuals to be corrupt?

1. 'Acquisition or gathering possessions' presents a basis for the motivation behind the acquisition of wealth.
2. The need for power and control over others.
3. Psychological need/psychopathic personality. The balances in their bulging bank accounts were of no practical import or intent—they merely satisfy their psychopathological need.
4. Socialisation. A child learns good morals/behaviours, but social influence and social acceptance of corruption desensitise their morals. Through socialisation, they learn that corruption is a widespread behaviour and that there is an approval of this problem behaviour; thus they get habituated to corrupt acts. Once the threshold is crossed by a small act, it is easier to commit bigger

acts. People who engage in negative behaviours will typically seek to justify their behaviours by denial of responsibility or denial of injury so they do not feel conflicted.

5. Humans have a tendency towards self-serving biases, leading to unethical behaviour. (Johns 1999, Moore and Loewernstein 2004). People develop 'learned helplessness' when they fail to escape from repeated corrupt acts. An escape from unpleasantness. Thus, despite such anger toward corruption, there also appears to be a sense of helplessness in doing something about it.

Organisational

Here are some of the factors or phenomenon that affects corruption in organisations.

Everybody is doing it. When some individuals in an organisation behave corruptly, others may imitate them, perhaps because they also come to view the behaviour as acceptable or simply because they think that everyone else is doing it. Anticorruption campaigns should be complemented with social campaigns centred on the morality of corruption, humanising the problem on an individual level.

Social proof. Some people's moral disposition changes when they become part of a corrupt group. Their personalities then change to conform to the group. They do not speak against a difficult or ambiguous situation because they take cues from others in the vicinity on how to act (Cialdini 1993). Thanks to the 'bystander effect', people tend not to speak up or act in response to a stressful situation if they perceive that no one else witnessing that situation is speaking up or acting (Latané and Darley 1970). The assumption that somebody else will do something about it leads to nobody doing anything. Another phenomenon is 'pluralistic ignorance', in which some individuals assume that others are silent for the same reasons that they are; they conclude that these others think that the act is an acceptably moral one and keep silent for that reason (Darley 2005). This ensures the silence of people who do not receive or give bribes even as others continue supporting the corrupt scheme.

Reciprocation. A powerful behavioural influence that indicates, 'We should try to repay, in kind, what another person has provided us' (Cialdini 1993). A concept of 'if you help me, I will help you'. Money is often given to help an official's personal need to get official favour.

Scarcity phenomenon. When in business negotiations, a business proposition may be deemed an opportunity not to miss. People look at gain rather than consequences. In business negotiations, scarcity can become a malign influence on decision making, as pressure to close the deal and concern for losing a scarce opportunity can draw negotiators into offering favours to improperly obtain or retain business.

Nohira (2015) noted, 'Research shows that when we are under extreme time pressure, we are more likely to behave unethically' and that likelihood may be increased by 'loss aversion', an unconscious bias that makes people weight losses more heavily than gains (Kahneman 2011).

The individual's judgement may be affected by the perception that there are rivals trying to access the same scarce resource (perception of a competition).

Decision-making. People's overreliance on faulty intuition and mental shortcuts rather than rational decision-making can lead them to condone or participate in corruption. Intuitive decision-making leads to corruption. Intuition is the ability to grasp a situation or information without the need for reasoning. Sometimes referred to as gut feeling, it is the opposite of rational decision-making, in which analytics, facts, and a step-by-step process are used to come to a decision. Intuition often relies on mental shortcuts "hardwired" into human behaviour.

Innate overconfidence in our decisions. One of the more fundamental biases that appear 'hardwired' into humans is the overconfidence effect: a bias in which a person's subjective confidence in his or her judgments is reliably greater than the objective accuracy of those judgments (Pallier et al. 2002). This happens in business decisions, but it can also warp self-perception on ethical issues. 'Moral overconfidence' is the gap 'between how people believe they would behave and how they actually behave,' which 'tends to be most evident in high-pressure situations, when there is some inherent ambiguity, when there are competing claims on our sense of right and wrong, and when our moral transgressions are incremental, taking us down a slippery slope' (Nohria 2015).

Corrupt communication/off-record indirect speech (ORIS). This is the way people in organisations carry out day-to-day business without mentioning words like 'bribe' or 'pay-off', which may incriminate them. 'The phenomenon in which a speaker says something he doesn't literally mean, knowing that the hearer will interpret it as he intended' (Pinker 2007). In the context of bribery, the use of ORIS means more than simply using euphemisms for 'bribe'; it requires that the speaker frame a statement or question in a way that provides both the speaker and the listener with plausible deniability should the listener be offended or angered by the speaker's implicit offer. Phrases like 'commitment' or 'management fees'. 'Taking care of the executive when he next visits; he is a supporter of the running project.'

ORIS can sometimes play a role in intra-organisational efforts to deter responsible conduct by other employees. An example: A financial employee emailed the manager that there is no proof or justification for making a payment. The manager called the finance employee and said, 'If you want to have several people put in jail, you should continue to send emails as you did earlier in the day,' and further instructed her to delete all emails regarding the payment. Note, he did not dispute the employee's observation but simply pointed out that the line of inquiry might have consequences for others and to avoid that to delete the emails.

It is important that organisations recognise the two types of 'cultures of compliance', with the law and the organisational culture described above that result in compliant behaviour that further violates the law. Companies should be aware of these psycho-social evidences in combating corruption in their organisation. Organisations should consider how to incorporate this information into their ethical and anticorruption training materials and courses so that individuals can more clearly recognise those sources of improper influence when they arise and provide explicit strategies on how to respond in ways other than tacit acceptance without protest.

6

A Political Culture of Corruption

This is a culture which focuses on getting rich and not to serve. It keeps the politician out of the service focus on to self-enrichment. This results in appropriate legislation not being made, and fraudulent contract awards are rife.

It is about uncontrolled power which is lorded over the citizens. It does not tolerate freedom of speech and clamps down on it by intimidation/ assassination of opponents. This hinders the population from a general uprising for fear of being a victim and with no recourse to fair justice. This culture has no element of humility, and it distances itself from the people it is meant to serve. There is no focus on accountability to the electorate. Legislative checks and balances are ignored and bypassed. There is an interwoven web of corruption and favour owing among politicians. None can escape and try to be honest. Anybody that does not toe the line is disgraced and eliminated.

Due to their corrupt nature, these politicians surround themselves with relatives and fellow corrupted individuals, usually of the same tribe or political region. This does not allow capable individuals to hold office, and it regionalises appointments to key official positions. This reflects on the performance and efficiency of the government.

These politicians have no leadership qualities and vision for the country. They do not lead by example. Hence, corruption filters down the line to the people. There is no effective governance, and if one is in place, it is ignored.

The other arm of the government, law enforcement agencies, is also corrupted and has no focused leadership. There is no effective law enforcement, politicians get away with their corrupt activities, and the citizens have no protection from criminals and no recourse to an effective justice system.

This is not a culture of leadership but of lordship over the citizens and does not tolerate differing views or opposition. These are brutally suppressed. The politicians will do anything and get away with it because the intimidated population is fear ridden and there is a lack of (or corrupt) law enforcement agencies. The political culture appoints corrupt individuals (or puppets) to key public positions. By so doing, it consolidates its position and prevents opposition.

Bribery is rife at the legislative houses. It is reported that highly paid members of a legislative assembly still expect a bribe. Members of a committee get generous travel and subsistence allowances to visit institutions all over the nation for assessment of their work and grant needs. The members of this committee are expected to be lavishly entertained when they visit and are also given a cash envelope in their pack. Failure to do this results in an unfavourable report, or a delay in approval (or reduction in amount) of the running grant, for that institution. This mirrors what happens at all levels of government and in the society in general.

Members of the legislative assemblies are given money and other gifts to sway their votes on certain laws and regulations, even budget approvals. There is often regional or ethnic affiliation within these legislative bodies. Appropriate legislation is not passed, and processes and funding are delayed. The ability of individuals, with collaborators, to dip into government funds and transfer them abroad or for personal use is common. These monies, if appropriately used in the country, will improve the quality of life of the citizens.

Appointment into key offices depends on who you know or are affiliated with, rather than on merit and qualifications. This results in poor governance and inefficiency in government institution. The favour is expected to be returned, usually by cash gift or awarding of contracts. Decisions are frequently influenced by the person who facilitated the appointment. Who you know gets you a job, a promotion, or a top government appointment.

Award of government contracts is another area where corruption and public fund embezzlement happens. Being awarded a government contract is regarded as a passport to becoming rich. Award of contracts is at the discretion of the minister or whoever is in charge. There are no contract award bodies that do this fairly and on merit. The costs of projects are highly inflated and given to the less qualified candidate (who sometimes subcontracts the project). Money from the project is given to those who facilitated the contract award, and down the line in order to get the paperwork done and the money released. Many projects are unfinished and nobody persecutes the contractor. Regional government embarks on grandiose and expensive projects to the detriment of the basic needs of the population—in some cases, non-payment of salaries for months.

The corrupt political culture, though it sounds horrid, occurs in some very corrupt parts of the world. Corruption also exists in other developed parts of the world; referred to with fanciful names such as 'money laundering', 'tax avoidance', and 'conduct unbecoming of a person in public office'. In these countries, the effects do not directly affect people's lives as they do in developing countries. There have been various scandals over the years about subtle use of political power, scandals involving claiming and use of parliamentary allowances, big corporations, and contract awards and implementation issues. The anticorruption measures in place vary from country to country in Europe. The concept of who you know, or what school you attended, gets you into jobs and appointments, if qualified.

7

Law Enforcement

Corruption breeds highly where there is a weak law enforcement and judiciary system. Often these agencies are corrupt. The criminal and the corrupt know that the chances of being caught are slim, and if caught, they can get away with it through corrupt law officers.

The police are well respected for their professionalism, efficiency, and impartiality when enforcing the law, protecting the people, and maintaining law and order. In a corrupt society, they cannot do their job well when it suits a corrupt government not to have an effective police system. The police become corrupted by politicians. Police officers are not well paid and funded, and the funds available are misused and find their way into corrupt officer's pockets. Police officers on the ground join the population norm and become corrupt and may openly demand a bribe to do their job. This state of affairs is frustrating to the population. The police community relations and cooperation from the public break down. The police must regain the confidence and trust of the population.

Police corruption and inappropriate behaviour can occur in various ways. Here are some examples:

1. An officer who arrests a criminal but uses the power of discretion to obtain money for personal use.
2. An officer using powers to access or destroy records when his relatives are involved.

3. A senior officer ordering his officers not to investigate an alleged act of a politician who is influential and friendly to the police cause.

4. An officer acting in a racial or prejudicial manner towards an alleged offender. This includes the use of excessive force.

5. Activities leading to perversion, obstruction, or diversion of the aim of justice.

6. Diversion of police resources for personal use or to projects not directly involved with police work.

7. Officers colluding with criminals in operations such as robbery, drug trafficking, tampering with evidence to obtain conviction, or lying about the circumstances of an arrest.

8. Getting of kickbacks from various sources, people, or companies that they are involved with in the course of doing their job.

9. The use of police resources for personal or other non-police-related organisational use.

The effects of inadequate law enforcement include

1. Increase in crime rate due to delay in crime investigation and delay in effecting justice. This leaves the criminal in the community where they can commit more crimes. The community does not feel safe.

2. Lack of trust and confidence in the police. There is a breakdown of the police/community relations.

3. Lack of traffic enforcement. People get away with breaches of road traffic regulations, because they can bribe their way out. Vehicle and driving licensing and checks when corrupted result in danger on the road and increased risk of accidents.

4. Poor recruitment of good quality candidates. People do not want to be part of an institution of bad repute.

Actions:

1. Do not elect a government that has no plans to eradicate corruption.
2. Do not elect a party that has no definite plan to reform and produce an effective police force.
3. Get involved in a police improvement commission (or similar body), as one of the lay members the voice of the people will be heard.
4. Get rid of corrupt officers by compulsory resignation or by sacking them.
5. Better training, education, and equipment for the police to do their job. Policing is a professional job. Higher qualification of entry at the basic level with adequate remuneration is essential. Their job is physically and mentally challenging. They require skills to enable them do their jobs. These include ability to multitask, physical stamina, exercising good judgement, perception, and leadership skills. Police forces must tackle the culture of in-house malpractice by training directed explicitly at those practices. Encouraging and rewarding reporting of corruption and other improper practices. Recruits must be taught to recognise the red flags of corruption and how the serious consequences of corrupt action affect their jobs. This recognition may be a preventative measure against corruption.
6. Appointment of senior police officers should be by merit, experience, and other criteria to ensure effective leadership. It should never be done on political, ethnic, or other nonfactual basis.

The judiciary has sadly also been corrupted. As with the police, it helps to reinforce corruption because the corrupt get away with their evil deeds and can bribe their way out. This is frustrating to the general public who cannot get justice. The actions to be taken are similar to those with the police. The corrupt judges must be retired or sacked. Replace them with honest, principled judges. Appointment of judges should also be on merit and factual defined criteria, not made by politicians and not based on ethnic or political affiliations.

8

Money, Politics, and Corruption

Money is any item or verifiable record that is generally
accepted as payment for goods and services and repayment of
debts in a particular country or socio-economic context
—Wikipedia, 'Money'

Its history evolved from trade by barter, dating back to 100,000 years to the development by many cultures, a form of exchange. The shekel in Mesopotamia in 3000 BC was a unit of weight, the use of shells by societies in America, Africa, Asia, and Australia. This was followed by the use of gold and silver around 300 BC. It is thought by modern scholars that these first stamped coins were minted around 650–600 BC. Gold and silver merchants issued a form of receipt redeemable for the money deposited. These gradually became accepted as a means of payment and were used as money. Paper money, or banknotes, was reportedly first used in China in the seventh century. They were used alongside the promissory notes and coins. Banknotes were first issued in Europe in Sweden by Banco Stockholm in 1661 and were used alongside the coins and promissory notes.

The gold standard as a monetary system where the medium of exchange are paper notes that are convertible into pre-set, fixed quantities of gold, replaced the use of gold coins as currency in the seventeenth to nineteenth centuries in Europe. These were made legal tenders, and people were discouraged from redeeming them into gold coins. All countries had adopted the gold standard paper notes by the beginning of the twentieth century. After the Second World War and the United Nation's Bretton Woods Conference, held in July 1994, most countries adopted fiat currencies that were fixed to the United States Dollar. The US dollar was in turn fixed to gold. Each country has its money supply, notes, and coins, which are legal tender.

Money functions as a mode of exchange, a common measure of value (a unit of account), a standard of value, and a store of value (can be saved, stored, and retrieved). Money is an essential commodity/tool needed in everyday life and has evolved into the electronic age where you may not need to carry coins and paper notes about. You only need a plastic card. Money is now moved across the world electronically. Money is not evil, but 'the love of money is the root of all kinds of evil' (1 Tim. 6:10 NKJV). Note that greed and temptation are accomplices. Greed and love of money have a part in corruption, but the concept of money itself may be corrupting. Psychologists in a research study have shown that when the concept of money was introduced in a business game (previously played without money), people's behaviour changes. 'What was happening with our participants is that the exposure to the concept of money was actually affecting the way they were thinking', Smith-Crowe said. 'The money cues were triggering a business decision mind frame, which meant that they focused on a cost-benefit analysis as motivation to pursue their own self-interest rather than thinking about things more broadly.' Her publication 'Seeing Green: Mere exposure to money triggers a business decision frame and unethical outcomes' in the May 2013 issue of *Organizational Behaviour and Human Decision Processes,* concludes, 'Mere exposure to money triggers a business decision frame and unethical outcomes.'

We are consciously and subtly being bombarded by the need to have money, to borrow if you do not have, to buy now and pay later. We enhance our status by buying the latest model of a gadget or phone. These are subtle cues as to how money can have a big effect on our decisions and our behaviour. We feel as if we know right from wrong, but we have to recognise that we're affected by things without realising it. Some say it is power that corrupts and that money is a portable form power. The need for power and status is in our genes and is seen in the primitive animal, who is preoccupied with power and social status. This determines many things—who it mates with, its hierarchy in the group. It turns out that merely thinking about money makes people more apt to engage in unethical behaviour, like lying, cheating, and stealing, according to researchers. People think about money as the end, not as a tool. Thinking about and putting money above all things drives a person to corruption and may lead to the development of a callous attitude in the process.

Greed plays a role, as does laziness. The concept that praying and hoping for a miraculous delivery of money, as preached by some pastors, should be discouraged. Hard work and entrepreneurship is required to create wealth. As another pastor said, God provides the tree. He will not build chairs, tables, etc., for you. The concept of getting rich quickly rather than by hard work tempts people into corruption. Having enough money and to be able to afford one's needs makes life comfortable. Entrepreneurs who make their money over years and through hard work know the value of money and spend vast amount of their money to work for the benefit of others, in eradication of disease, poverty and for the benefit of the human race. In contrast money laundered and acquired through corrupt means are stored in banks and other places. Money is meant to be used for the benefit of others. Though people may have the satisfaction of riches, there are many things that money cannot buy.

Money and Politics

Politicians need money to contest elections and achieve power. The politician is sponsored by individuals and companies and when in power uses public funds to repay sponsors and is likely to be influenced by the sponsors in decision making. In some countries, where money is the barometer of how much power people can have, people will acquire money by corrupt means. The relationship between money, politics, and power is hard to separate. Money is needed to campaign for election into politics and achieve power; power and other factors corrupt and allow diversion of public money into personal wealth.

It is therefore essential that (1) businesses and personal financing of political parties campaign be regulated. Disclosure of campaign funds is essential; (2) there be limits to corporate and individual contributions to ensure that democracy is not for sale.

A publication by Transparency International, 'Money, Politics, and Power: Corruption risk in Europe 2012', Looks at the problem in various European countries and reveals variations in the control mechanisms to prevent corruption. In developing countries, in particular, there should be control mechanisms in place to be open about and to limit campaign funds for parties and individuals. Declaration of assets on assumption of office and mechanisms should be in place to avoid misuse of public funds. Politicians are custodians of public money, which is to be used for the benefit of the population or country. People should be able to challenge the unlawful use of public money. Improvements in the law-enforcing and judiciary systems are a deterrent to corruption. Sporadic external audits of government departments (or individuals) are detectors of corruption and may act as a deterent. Improvement in education level and in the national ethic to hard work and money will help to reduce the incidence of corruption.

9

Power and Corruption

The word power comes from the Latin word *potere*, which means 'to be able'.

Definitions: the ability or capacity to do something or act in a particular way; the capacity or ability to direct or influence the behaviour of others or the course of events; possession of control, authority, or influence others.

Leadership has power and influence at its core. They get things done. Power of leadership is social power to make decisions that benefit us all as a society. This is the type we want our elected leaders to have. Personalised power is used for personal gain, at the detriment of others. The two forms of power are interwoven. Often the socialised power is used but in the process there is personal gain. The problem arises when the personal gain is greater and is to the detriment of the society.

Power can cause leaders to 'assume an attitude of exception making' when they think the rules of good behaviour does not apply to them. After all, they are serving the people and they are doing a good job. Leaders often become 'power intoxicated' and engage in wrong behaviour because they can get away with it. Their followers are willing to collude with them and make exceptions because they are the leader.

Other types of power include divine power, parental power, and power resulting from industrial wealth.

Personal power comes from our experiences, skill, and knowledge, and referent power comes from being trusted and respected. We can gain referent power when others trust what we do and respect us for how we handle situations. Personal power is different from formal power, which is as a result of one's position as the head or boss.

Advantages of power include allowing leaders to be assertive and confident in making decisions and following a course of action. That is using power to 'get the job done'.

On the negative side, the more powerful people become, the more they focus on their own selfish objectives and the less able they are to see other people's perspective.

Some individuals are power hungry and become 'leaders from hell', using their powers to oppress others.

A series of experiments found that once honest people had tasted power, they couldn't resist rewarding themselves at the expense of others. The taste of power seems to induce the appetite, and the more they want, the less they want to let go.

Strong governance mechanisms and strong institutions are the keys to keeping leaders in check. There should be a limit to how much leaders can drink from the power cup.

Power has two characteristics—it is coercive and persuasive.

Coercive power is held with the threat of sanctions or force. It influences decision making by taking something away as punishment.

Persuasive power comes through the process of solicitation, convincing, and arguing, without violence or threats.

There are four ways to use power.

1. **Force**. Power involving physical means. This style shuts down contributions from others.
2. **Persuasion**. Act of trying to convince someone. Use of influence.
3. **Manipulation**. Managing or influencing someone or something, skilfully to one's advantage. Discretionary control over resources such as money, equipment, information, and space can be used to build power
4. **Exchange**. The use of power through incentives. 'I want you to do something for me. To convince you to do it, I will offer you something that you value.'

In companies, as in governments, people reward those who help them and punish those who stand in their way. These four power modes can be used to various extents by people in power or politics, either legally or illegally, or as a means to corruption.

To be in a position of power is a privilege. The position of power should be used with reflection, wisdom, and maturity and for the purpose that the power is bestowed.

Effective use of power involves

1. Concentrating on our personal powers.
2. Ability to listen and learn from others.
3. Thinking beyond the box.
4. Application of a personal touch, being generous and being visible. Put aside resentments, jealousies, anger, and anything else that might hinder you.
5. Good communication, carrying people along with you, and clarifying expectations helps effective use of power.
6. Dealing effectively with opposition, not by bulldozing them but by pursuing your goals and trying to build relationships. Be ready to make the first move that catches the opposition by surprise. Convince and bring the opposition on board. Remove them as a last resort by offering them a position suited to their aspirations.
7. Exercising power becomes more effective when you align your goal with a socially viable objective.

10

Your Rights as a Citizen

In any country, you as a citizen have basic rights to which you are entitled. Rights are the fundamental rules about what is allowed or owed to people. Rights are one of the pillars of the society. The rights which we enjoy today have centuries of history of people and societies demanding and eventually obtaining those rights. It is the duty of politicians, or those in government, to ensure that citizens' rights are provided and protected. These rights are published widely and should be in the laws of the country.

Citizens have the right to

1. Be respected, irrespective of colour, race, ethnicity sex, religion, etc.
2. Live and be protected by the laws of the land
3. Have equal rights with other citizens. Not to be discriminated against on any basis (race, ethnicity, religion, gender)
4. Practice religion without persecution and without domination, intimidation, or persecution by anybody, other religions, or government
5. Freedom of speech and freedom of expression
6. Justice and to protection under the law
7. Basic infrastructure amenities—light, water, sanitation, roads, housing
8. Health and social facilities (a healthy nation is a wealthy one)
9. Basic education

10. The right to vote and to be voted for

Societies that have these rights established and practically enforced are less likely to go on a corrupt path.

Actions

As advised in other sections of this book, be involved at the grassroots political level. Elect good politicians who are accountable and who will ensure that all government departments function well and without corruption, a government that will assure these rights are available to you. There are no rights without responsibilities. Every citizen must carry out his or her responsibilities as a good citizen, obey the laws of the land, and be honest. Respect the view and rights of others and be prepared to fight for your rights and theirs. Be ready to defend these rights if they are infringed. Stand up against corruption, expose it, and help to eradicate it.

11

Politics, Politician, and Political Parties

Politics is defined as activities associated with the governance of a country or area; processes of making decisions and organised control over human communities, particularly a state. It is the activities of the government, members of the law-making organisation, or people who influence the way a country is governed.

People go into politics to serve and to make a change and improve the lives of their country and its citizens. Any reasons apart from that are suspect and should be questioned. People can go into politics because of the power and status it gives them, while others (especially in corrupt countries) do so to acquire wealth. You can respect the office or the position of the president, but the president or politician has to earn the respect of his country by their performance in office and the care and respect that he or she has for the country.

Assess Your Politicians—People You Elected to Govern

What have they done since they were elected? How many debates have they contributed to? How many good laws have they proposed and affected? Are they communicating with you very well? Is their constituency offices active? Do they hold meetings, public or private, with those who elected them, to discuss issues that concern their communities? Politicians are accountable to the electorate, and they are not above the law.

A politician must have a basic level of morals, decency, and integrity.

What useful information can you get from their website or social media? Their plans for the community, how they are effecting the plans—in the legislative houses or parliament?

You elected the politicians to serve you, not to lord over you, and you did not elect them to do nothing. Would you employ a person to do a job and pay him a good salary and a generous allowance to do nothing? So he could insult you and steal from you? Make your life difficult and make you poorer. Would you re-elect such a person?

Does the politician have a job description and responsibilities? Yes he does. Is it written down and well publicised? How many of them actually do their jobs according to specifications, honestly and with integrity? You assess a public official by these criteria, and if they do not meet them, do not re-elect them. Don't re-elect a politician because he gives you peanut during his election campaign or because he comes from your tribe or region but rather because of his vision for the state, his vision to make your life and the lives of your children/grandchildren better and to make your country great.

It is vital that you have a platform to speak to politicians before, during, and after their election.

A politician must have

1. Willingness and ability to serve.
2. The requisite skills, experience, and good track record in professional or public life.
3. Literacy. They will need to read documents and reports and attend meetings at which important decisions need to be made.
4. Honesty, integrity, and respect for the rule of law.
5. The ability to learn, listen, work in and lead a team, and make good decision based on facts and rational thinking. A politician must have good communication skills and be a good negotiator.
6. A written vision of how he sees his country and how he wants to serve the people and contribute to making it a better place to live. He must have a team of people who share his values and aspirations and who will work with him to achieve these aims.

7. Respect for the feelings, wishes, and rights of others. This quality is essential for a politician or anybody in a position of authority or leadership. In fact, this is a quality that has to start at a very early age in the home and reinforced in primary and secondary education.

A politician that has no respect for his or her country and people is not fit to hold office. Among other things, lack of respect for the people they are supposed to serve leads to an inability to make good legislation, treatment of people with contempt, and the impression that the politician is lording power over the people. They are likely to be corrupt and thrive in a corrupt society. No politician or a group of politicians from an ethnic or geographical region should attempt to pass legislation which favours them and marginalises other groups. The job of politicians is to serve the people and work towards the prosperity of their country and the unity of their people.

Why do you belong to a political party?

1. You support the party's aims and goals and because you want them to achieve them.
2. It gives you a feeling of being involved in your country's government. This allows you to express an agenda or opinion regarding the direction of the country.
3. It gives you the chance to gain friendships and other social opportunities, personal status from being a member of the party.
4. It provides personal gains, social and business contacts, an opportunity to be elected as a candidate.

Role of Political Parties

1. Selection of candidates to run for office. They must examine their candidates closely to see what their position and track records are and to ensure they are fit for office.
2. Keeping other political parties in check. Reporting suspicious behaviour to the public attention helps balance the scales of power.

3. Keeping the public informed at the local, national, and international level about issues that affect the people and the nation.
4. Organising the government of the country when in power and keeping other political parties in check when in opposition.
5. Broadly representing various groups across the country (not an ethnic or regional base).

The change starts with you. The system as it is will not change unless we all determine to change it.

Actions

1. Do you belong to a party? If not, why? Consider having a say in the issues that concern you by joining one.
2. Does your party have processes in place for selection of candidates who run for office? Do you have a say, and is it democratic? If candidate selection is imposed for other reason and not on merit, then work towards making a change.
3. Discuss what you want to change with others and be determined to make the changes.
4. Educate the party members and the public.
5. Expose corrupt practices an aim to make a change. Ensure that processes are in place to make your party governs without corruption.
6. Ensure that your party has an anticorruption policy document in place.
7. You do not have to re-elect the current politicians who are part of the corrupt system. They are not likely to change.
8. Encourage and recruit younger people members into the parties.
9. Younger people who are honest and committed to making a change can form their own party.

12

Qualities and Skills for Politicians and Public Office Holders

People in politics and public offices are responsible for the smooth running of the affairs of a country or institutions. They will have to make decisions that affect the lives of people and the country in general. They will be responsible for handling huge amounts of money and making sure that this is spent appropriately and for the benefit of the population at large. The quality and vision of the politicians determine what laws are passed and which processes are effected to improve the country, to make it great. These great responsibilities should not be handed to those who are not qualified or who are incapable. Therefore, there must be qualities and attributes that are expected of such office holders.

To be a successful politician you need to possess certain skills and surround yourself with a team that helps with those skills.

Gerald Ferris, a management and psychology professor at Florida State University, says that 'behaviours that are genuine, authentic, straightforward, and effective are associated with political savvy. Leaders who are not politically skilled come off as manipulative or self-serving'. A good politician should have the following skills and qualities. These are important if they are going to be effective in doing their jobs well.

1. **Honesty.** Honesty is quality or fact of being honest, upright, fairness, truthful, sincerity, not deceitful. This quality in a person builds credibility and trust which are foundations that will build confidence and respect of the people

2. **Communication skills**
    - Public Speaking and presentation skills.
    - Research and writing skills
    - Use of the media, especially social media
    - Thinking before speaking. Politically skilled managers have impulse control. They tend to choose their organisational battles wisely and size up situations before deciding how to present ideas to others.
    - Good networking. Those who possess a strong networking ability build friendships and beneficial working relationships by garnering support, negotiating, and managing conflict. Skilled networkers know when to call on others and are seen as willing to reciprocate.

3. **Problem-solving and crisis-management skills**
    - Analytical skill. Identifying the best solution in the national interest (not on party loyalty).
    - Evaluation and rectification. Determine if an apology, explanation, and public support are needed in a crisis situation.

4. **An understanding of the people that they serve**
    - Perceptive observers of others and of social situations.
    - Comprehension social interaction, accurately interpretation of their own behaviour as well as that of others.
    - Strong powers of discernment and high self-awareness.
    - Respect for the people they serve.
    - Influence and good rapport; an ability to form harmonious relationships with the people they serve and to understand their feelings and ideas and to be able to relate well to these.

5. **Sincerity.** Politically skilled individuals display high levels of integrity, authenticity, sincerity, and genuineness. They are, or

appear to be honest, open, and forthright, inspiring trust and confidence.

6. **Compassion**. A humane quality to see and understand the suffering of others and wanting to do something to alleviate that suffering. Good political leaders use their compassion to see the need of the people they serve and to determine the best steps that will benefit those affected.

7. **Integrity** (honesty and uprightness). The highest standard of integrity is required. This allows trust because he or she will not veer from values even if it benefits them to do so.

8. **Confidence**. Constituents must believe that they will act in a right, proper and effective way. Confidence to inspire and to motivate others to get things done.

9. **Flexibility.** Give and take of politics, and ability to find common ground. Good listening skill to all arguments and opinions and to learn what it takes to reach a consensus.

10. **Service.** The aim of going into politics is to serve and make a difference to the lives of the people and for the good of the country. The politician should love his or her country and have a passion for making a difference. They must work hard and have a good work ethic. They must possess a personal belief that hard work and diligence have a moral benefit and reward. When the head of an institution believes this, he or she can influence the whole organisation or unit. Good managerial skill is desirable. This helps a manager organise their work and manage their staff or department if they are ministers.

It may be difficult to find an individual possessing all the professional skills needed to be a successful politician; hence, in some systems, government or political are given budget allowances to employ advisers, press officers, etc. In corrupt situations, these monies are pocketed by politicians, and there is no accountability for their use.

13

The ABCs of Standing Up against Corruption

<u>A</u>

Awareness of the issues about corruption and how it affects society is essential.

Anticorruption Measures must be put in place in all works of life.

Arrange groups, to tackle corruption. Join an anticorruption group to educate yourself and to make a change.

Appoint only qualified and honest people into public office.

Accountability. Politicians and holders of public offices must be accountable to the people. Working within rules and regulation must be able to justify their decisions.

Achievers and hard workers should be esteemed and not people who get rich by corrupt means.

Appointment into public offices should be by merit not by who you know.

Award of contracts must be reviewed. It should be transparent and done by a panel that adheres to strict guidelines and to national pricing guidelines.

Anticorruption education. This is essential to teach students about the negative effects of corruption. Industries should educate their employees about corruption and encourage whistleblowing.

Attitude of our citizens to many things must change (attitude to work, money, law and order, respect for each other and our rights, punctuality).

<u>B</u>

Be aware.

Be vigilant about corruption. People use power for individual gain (corruption).

Bribery is a major aspect of corruption. Be against bribery.

Be assertive if a bribe is demanded of you. Ask for the regulation that requires the payment, and decline to pay the bribe. Advise that you may need to report it to your employer or law enforcing agents. At work, you must challenge any request for you to act improperly or fraudulently.

Be encouraged to join or form a local anticorruption group.

BED. Be involved, Expose, and Do something about corruption.

Best people, who are qualified and honest, should be appointed to public offices.

Be honest and truthful in all that you do.

Basic human rights and needs must be accorded to every citizen. Housing, electricity, clean water, education, justice, and a sanitary environment are basic rights of every citizen.

<u>C</u>

Condemn corruption. Campaign against it.

Compassion/care. Have compassion on your fellow men that are affected by corruption. Compassion is a quality desirable for politicians and anybody in authority.

Close loopholes in the law. Close the door to corruption.

Corruption does no good to anybody. Resolve to eliminate it.

Companies and contractors must demonstrate that they have an anticorruption policy in place. This must be functioning and it must be verifiable. The consequences of a breach of the government anticorruption policy must be clear and include exclusion from government contracts.

Change starts by doing things differently. To fight corruption you have to do things differently. We cannot keep doing the same things and expect a change.

D

Demand your rights if a bribe are demanded. Ask for the regulations that allow for the payment.

Decline a bribe or other forms of corruption, advise the briber that you are bound to report it to your employers or the law enforcement agents (according to your workplace anticorruption policy).

Do not give in to corruption.

Drive out corrupt people from office.

Desire to build a corruption-free society by passing, enforcing, and monitoring anticorruption legislation.

Do not bribe your way into jobs, offices, or positions. Make sure that you qualify for it, by your qualification and experience.

Discipline yourself.

Do not glorify the rich, corrupt, and wealthy individuals but reward and esteem those who contribute positively into society.

Demand the institution or company's customer service and anticorruption policies, especially if you think a delay in getting a service is because you have not offered a bribe.

Do your work diligently and well, without expecting to be bribed to do it.

Discuss corruption at your work or business. Identify the corrupt individuals and put in place anticorruption measures.

E

Expose and report corruption. Whistleblowers must be given legal protection.

Enforce anticorruption regulation. Eliminate corrupt people/officials from public office.

Eliminate situations that foster corruption, by training, putting good governance in place.

Establish and enforce anticorruption legislation.

Encourage good work ethics.

Educate all the members of the community about corruption, its effects, and how to eradicate it.

Educate yourself. Apply for jobs on your own merit, not by bribing your way in.

Ensure that you vote in honest, capable people who have a national vision into political office.

Employers should have an anticorruption policy in place. They should train workers about what to do if a bribe or other corrupt practices are offered to them.

Every institution or government office that offers public service should have a customer services document and an anticorruption policy.

F

Face the facts. Corruption does anyone no good. Make a stand against corruption and make your country corruption free.

Free your country of corruption

Fight Corruption at all levels of your society. Nobody but we citizens must start the move.

Fill public offices with qualified, honest people who have good work ethics.

Financial transactions. Both government and private institutions must comply with a anticorruption/money laundering legislation, which must identify and trace the original source of the money. Transactions that fail the laid down criteria must be reported by lawyers, customs and excise, or government department involved.

G

Government should lead the fight against corruption. Anticorruption should be driven from the top.

Government Offices and institutions should be a model where legislation, training, enforcing, and monitoring of corruption must happen.

Government institution and offices that serve the public must have a customer service document and an anticorruption policy document.

Government appointees, employees, and contractors must be trained and be aware of anticorruption, policies, and laws. The consequences of a breach should be made known.

Government contracts award systems must be reviewed. It should be transparent, done by a panel that adheres to strict guidelines and national pricing guidelines. This avoids over-inflation of contract award funds.

Gift Policy. Every government and private institutions must have a gift policy, which is widely circulated to customers. This discourages giving of gifts to the employee and defines what may be deemed a bribe. Company and government hospitality costs and gifts should be defined and limited. The Inland Revenue should have tax guidelines.

Good governance must be put in place at all levels of society.

Greed leads to corruption. Fight your greed if in office or a position of power.

H

Hard work and the will to be productive must be a culture of the society.

Health and productivity of the country is enhanced by the provision of the basic human needs (housing, clean water, sanitary environment, electricity, and food). This should be among the priorities of a good government.

Have the interest of the society, your country, at heart instead of your own self-interest.

I

Integrity is a virtue that the whole country must have. This must start in the home and at all levels of education.

Inland Revenue System. This government department should be more effective and alert. Not only for revenue generation in terms of taxes but also target individuals that contentiously display wealth at parties or live a lifestyle that is above their expected income.

Interest yourself in the politics of your country. You elected the politicians to govern, and you must have a say in whatever they are doing. Do not leave it to others.

Introduction of money into a situation influence how people think and behave. People in power should curb the natural instinct to make decisions in their own self-interest.

Invest time and money to educate yourself and the population.

J

Join an anticorruption group and make a difference. Join your local political party. You will be able to make a difference and make your views known. Encourage the young people to join the youth wing of their local political party. They can make a change and infuse new ideas into the parties.

Job creation should be encouraged, both by governments, entrepreneurs, and companies. It helps the economy.

K

Know your rights and demand them from your government. A government that denies you your rights should be denied your votes.

Knowledge. Knowledge is power. Get yourself educated about issues that affect you. And determine to say and do something about anything you are not happy about.

L

Looting of a country's treasury is not acceptable. Regulation and systems must be in place to prevent individuals and groups of politician from unlawful access. Do not esteem or glorify anybody who has acquired wealth through corrupt means.

Love of money is the root of all evils. Greed and temptation, when added, lead to corruption.

Let your vote do the talking. Let it work for you; use it wisely.

M

Manufacturing jobs are essential for a country's economy. A country that imports everything is dependent on others including their economic and currency fluctuation. Governments and entrepreneurs should be encouraged to create jobs.

Money mentality in the society must change. Respect the rich who earn his money by hard work, despise the corrupt rich, and do not admire or hero worship them. Money is meant to be used to benefit the society and not stacked up in local or foreign banks.

Monitor the activities and decision of politician or public officials to make sure they are lawful and ethical.

Management of public funds is a duty of politicians and people in authority. This should be safeguarded against corrupt individuals and groups. There should be guidelines about use of public money. The amount that an officer has unilateral power to disburse should be limited and monitored.

N

Nobody can stop corruption except us who are affected. Eradication starts with you. The current corrupt politicians will only pay lip service to eradication.

Never assume that others will do something about an issue that affects you and your community. Be part of the voice of change; join like-minded groups as a step to effecting a change. Bring the issue to the attention of your local member of parliament or of the state assembly and demand that they look into the issue.

Nobody is above the law. Politicians must be law-abiding and act within the law. They should set a standard. If they fall short must be prepared to, or forced to, resign.

Nip corruption in the bud. Where it has grown to a tree, uproot it. Plant a seed of honesty in its place.

O

Organisations, companies, and government departments and institution must have an operational anticorruption policy.

Oppose and expose any unlawful or illegal acts—in the government, in your workplace, and in the society.

Oath of Office. A statement (of key behaviour and responsibility) that is sworn by political officials at all levels, and also by key post holders in the military. It is essential that these post holders are accountable to the country and abide by these statements.

P

The police and other law-enforcement agencies have to be overhauled. A head of the police force, which is honest and ready to combat corruption, should be appointed. The police force needs to be well equipped and trained to do their job effectively.

Punctuality. Attitude to timekeeping must change in all aspects of life. Time lost cannot be recovered. Time is money. A country that runs punctually and on time is productive.

Political Parties should clean up their act to make them effective in office. This may involve vetting and training of members and those standing for election.

Provision of housing, electricity, clean water, food, and a sanitary environment are basic human needs and should be provided by governments.

Probity. The quality of having strong moral principles, honesty, and decency should be taught from homes, in school, and at all education levels until it becomes a quality of the whole population.

Power. Political and certain other positions have power and authority associated with them. Power is to be used to make decisions that benefit the society. Power should be exercised with wisdom, restraint, and common sense.

Q

Quality should be the aim in all aspects of life—in education, in government, in industry, in politics and in our personal lives. Don't accept mediocrity.

Query and be assertive about any request for you to act fraudulently or unlawfully.

R

Religious leaders must teach honesty, hard work, compassion, and the ill effects of corruption on the society. Prayers, though essential, are not a substitute to hard work, honesty, and integrity.

Responsibility. The attitude of responsibility must be taught to all citizens, right from the elementary school throughout the educational system. The population must be taught to expect people in office to be responsible and accountable.

Respect for the laws and regulations of the country. This must be taught, at all levels, until it becomes the norm in the country.

Respect for your fellow citizens and their rights.

S

Starts in the home. Eradication of corruption starts in the home. Teach your children, by your own examples, to be honest and to have respect and compassion for their fellow men. Discuss corruption and its ill effects with your children.

Starts with you. Eradication of corruption starts with you. It is our problem, and we have an active part in dealing with it. We cannot keep doing the same things and expect a change. Change starts by doing things differently.

Systemic disregard and noncompliant with rules and regulation by politicians and people in authority should no longer be tolerated.

Social media has become a useful tool in expressing opinions and for mobilising people against injustice and other issues. Beware of fake news and those who use it to foster discord and to fan the flames of old and traditional issues which may not be relevant today.

Service. The population and political parties need to be educated that holding public office is to serve the people. Abuse of privileges, power, and corruption should not be tolerated. Anybody that falls below the standards expected should be forced to resign.

T

Time is money. Time lost or wasted cannot be recovered. Teach your children and nation to have regards for time. Be punctual and be timely.

Teach. Teach qualities that lay the foundation against corruption to your children. Start in the home, in the schools, and at all levels of society.

Treat the corrupt and corruption with contempt. Treat honesty with respect.

The change starts with you. The system as it is will not change itself unless we all determine to change it.

Training. Government institutions, companies, and other organisations must train their staff about corruption: how to recognise factors and situations that may lead to corruption and how to deal with them. All must legislate anticorruption policies.

U

Understand how the government and governance systems in your country work. Do not be ignorant, educate yourself, and be more knowledgeable. Be more active in the political issues which affect you. Do not assume that somebody else will do something about it. Silence and indifference is a recipe for and fuel for the perpetuation of corruption

V

Vote. You have a vote; it is your voice in the running of your country's affairs. Vote for politician on their merit, not because they come from your tribe, they are the same religion as you, or they have been recommended by other politicians who are corrupt. You have to use your vote wisely. Use it to vote out corrupt politicians. Vote in change.

<u>W</u>

Whistleblowing policy should be in place in government, companies, and all institutions. Whistleblowers should be protected by law and should not be treated unfairly or lose their jobs.

<u>X</u>

Exercise your rights. Demand it from your government and your politicians at your local level and place of work. Respect other people's rights.

<u>Y</u>

Young people should get involved in the existing parties and make a change from within. Form your own party if necessary. Present yourselves as fresh candidates for election instead of the same old corrupt politicians who keep presenting themselves again and again.

<u>Z</u>

Zoom in on corruption and eradicate it.

14

Anticorruption Starts with You (the Cost of Corruption Affects You)

Cost of Corruption

It has been widely quoted that worldwide corruption (not just bribery) imposes annual costs to the global economy of approximately $2.6 trillion, roughly 5 per cent of global GDP (WEF June 2008). Your money, which could be used to develop the nation and make life better for all, is eaten up by corruption. 'Corruption creates and increases poverty and exclusion. While corrupt individuals with political power enjoy a lavish life, millions of Africans are deprived of their basic needs like food, health, education, housing, access to clean water and sanitation' (José Ugaz, Chair, Transparency International). The amount of money extorted and stolen each year from developing countries is over ten times the approximately $100 billion in foreign assistance being provided to them by all the governments and civil society organizations in the world (UNDP, December 2008).

World Bank research findings suggest that by tackling corruption and improving the rule of law, countries can increase their national incomes by 'as much as four times in the long term and child mortality can fall as much as 75 percent'. More than $1 trillion ($1,000 billion) are paid in bribes every year, as well as more than 3 per cent of world income in 2002 (World Bank Institute estimate).

- More than 70 per cent of small- and medium-sized enterprises (SMEs) in transition economies perceive corruption as an impediment to their business (Business Environment and Enterprise Performance Survey 2000).
- $148 billion leaves the African continent every year because of corruption (African Union estimates).

Reducing corruption should boost economic prosperity; corruption reduces GPD/capital, leading to a lower standard of living. Lower levels of perceived corruption are associated with higher levels of GDP per capita. High levels of corruption increase the cost of doing business. This is passed on to consumers. In 2015, a Transparency international survey in thirty-six African countries found that nearly 75 million Africans paid a bribe in the last one year. This is 22 per cent of public service users. The survey explored the views of citizens most affected most by corruption. What services had they paid bribes for? The survey looked at the level of corruption in the different institutions, groups, and society as a whole. It also explored why people do not report corruption.

Among its findings were that they perceive corruption to be rising and that their governments are not doing anything or failing in their effort to do something about it. Bribery affects more than one in five Africans, especially the poor in urban areas. The police and the courts have the highest rate of bribery. Many people feel unable to contribute to helping fight corruption. Only 38 per cent seem to think they can help.

It is therefore important that those of us affected by corruption pause, reflect, and strategise as to how we can fight corruption. The fight against corruption *starts* with you.

S

Start with yourself.

Start in your home, in your workplace

Start in the schools. Teach children sense of nationalism, honesty, integrity, and compassion.

Start an anticorruption group in your party or society.

Start processes (be involved) that educate the public, that improves the quality of law enforcement and legal justice systems, that improve governance.

Stop the culture of whom you know to get you along. Rather, depend on your own qualification, abilities, and experience. Shop this culture and expose it.

Self-regulation. Professional bodies (doctors, lawyers, accountants, engineers, teachers, etc.) should self-regulate to maintain professional ethics and integrity. They should discipline members who bring disrepute to their profession by being corrupt.

T

Treat an attempt to bribe you seriously. Threaten to report it and inform the Briber that it is illegal.

Take the time to do your job well, without expecting to be bribed.

Teach good work ethics.

There is no point grumbling about corruption and its effect on our lives if we keep voting in the same corrupt politicians.

The time to change is the next election. Use your vote wisely to elect good politicians.

The press and the media have a great role to play—to educate the people, to investigate, to and expose fraud and corruption.

The freedom of the press must be preserved.

A

Appoint the best people for the job. Stop the 'it's who you know' culture.

Appoint (vote in) politicians and leaders with integrity.

Anticorruption policy must be in place and displayed in all government offices and companies (by legislation).

Advice the bribe requester to tell you the regulation that requires you to pay what he/she is asking for.

Actively participate in the processes that help to improve the society and which help to eradicate corruption.

Accountability. Demand that your leaders and politician are accountable to you the people. Be accountable to the appropriate authorities in your job and if you hold public office, to the people.

Aim to be more assertive. Teach and encourage assertiveness in the society. This will help the people to challenge injustice, corruption, or anything that are not right or unlawful. Passivity allows corruption, injustice, and unlawful behaviour.

Assist 'gender egalitarianism' in the community. This is a concept that minimises the differences in roles of male and females in the home, organisation, and communities. Societies that do this have more women in position of authority, and this has been shown to lower corruption levels.

R

Report fraud and corruption. Be active in eradicating corruption.

Reform the law enforcement agencies and the judiciary. Appoint honest people to head the police force.

Respect and keep the laws of the country.

Resist an attempt to drag you into fraud. Receive no bribes if offered, threaten to report the offer.

Respect your neighbour and fellow countrymen. Respect and uphold their rights.

Respect a person for their work and contribution to society (not the money they have).

Request and ensure that your government provide the basic human needs and rights.

Reverse the 'power distance' in the community. This is a concept in which obedience toward superiors is expected and clearly distinguishes between those with status and power and those without. You do not have to obey an older or richer person if they demand inappropriate behaviour from you, just because society demands it. This reduces the level of corruption.

T

Tomorrow belongs to all of us (and our children); live today well.

Take time to educate yourself, your children, and your community.

Treat your fellow men with respect, kindness, and compassion.

Tact is needed to deal with the ignorant man.

The freedom of speech must be maintained.

The politicians and people in authority must not be allowed to use their power unlawfully. There must be legislation and checks in place to prevent abuse of power and misuse of public funds.

15

Steps to Take to Stand against Corruption in Public Office

Anticorruption must involve every citizen and be led by a reputable body/organisation. It is a targeted issue that must be monitored and reviewed regularly.

Processes to be put in place may include an anticorruption resources centre. This centre will have literature, policies, and processes available to prevent corruption and an online resource to tackle corruption in all situations. There should be a robust reporting and investigating system. There should be an education arm with facilities to hold conferences and which a wide variety of information leaflets translated to all the main languages in the country. These should be available online or by post on request.

Other areas to be looked at and effects positively are listed below.

Accountability. In leadership roles, officials must take responsibility for their actions, decisions, and policies and have an obligation to report and be answerable to the public for these. This must be engrained in all aspects of the nation and individual's life.

Transparency in all aspects of public life. This implies openness communication and accountability on the part of people who are in public office.

Whistleblowing. Adequate laws and regulations must be in place to allow whistleblowing. There must be legal protection for the whistleblower.

Civil service reform. Especially in developing countries should be affected to ensure smooth running of and delivery of government services. There should be an outline of the skills and behaviour expected of civil servants at all levels.

Financial and assets disclosure by public servants. This must be in effect to monitor and deter public officials from being corrupt and to deter self-enrichment.

Open contracting system. This must be transparent and accessible to the public. A system of payment by result and independent verification of work done for agreed payment (payment by result) should be the norm.

Integrity management. Should happen in businesses, and for individuals.

Bribery laws. The enforcement of anti-bribery laws is a priority. This will prevent the bribing of public and foreign officials and of the bribery by public and foreign companies.

Good governance. Describes how public institutions conduct public affairs and manage public resources. Governance is 'the process of decision-making and the process by which decisions are implemented (or not implemented)' (United Nations ESCAP publication, 'What Is Good Governance?'). The term *governance* can apply to corporate, international, national, or local governance, or to the interactions between other sectors of society. Good governance processes should be in place in all areas and aspects of the society. Good governance assures that corruption is minimised. It has eight major characteristics. It is participatory, consensus orientated, accountable, transparent, responsive (to the present and future needs of the society), effective and efficient, equitable and inclusive, and adherent to the rule of law.

Education of the society. More money should be spent on education. Improvement of literacy rate in the community should be the aim of a good government. Fostering of good Ethics in the society, by education and setting the standard of expected good behaviour.

16

Get Involved/Change Politics in Your Country/Your Vote Counts

A vote is a means, by which a preference is made known when issues need to be decided—that is to express a choice or an opinion. This may be in the form of raising hands and a count in favour of each issue or by indication on paper which is then counted. It is a fundamental basis of democracy. Voting is a process in which the people make their choices known, especially in politics. It is also known as an election and allows the people to make choices as to who represents them in the running of the affairs of their country. Voting can take place by various means, physically at the polling station, by post, or electronically. Whatever way a vote is cast, there are processes or bodies (e.g., electoral commission) that ensure fairness in the conduct of the election and verify results. The vote, which we take for granted today, has a long history among people of different economic backgrounds, ages, sexes, and racial backgrounds, fighting for a right to vote over centuries. It is, therefore, a right which individuals must exercise and use well. If you do not vote, you allow a minority who vote to determine the affairs of your nation. The vote must not be allowed to be corrupted or manipulated. Use your vote well.

You get the government you elect. You cannot elect corrupt politicians and expect an honest government. Plato said, 'One of the penalties for refusing to participate in politics is that you end up being governed by your inferiors.'

'Corruption breeds corruption.' A corrupt person needs other corrupt individuals to survive. A corrupt political party breeds corrupt politicians, and when the party is in power, it forms a corrupt government. Hence, you have the legislative house which is corrupt. A corrupt government is no good to a country. A corrupt government will not fight corruption. The political parties have a culture of nominating people who are corrupt or who can be manipulated or corrupted for office. It is up to you as an individual and for us as a community to stand up against corruption and to fight it.

1. Get involved in your party and make sure it has processes in place to train and nominate honest, hardworking people to stand for election. It is at the local party level that you can make an impact and effect changes. Involve the young people in the youth wings of political parties.
2. Elect politicians on merit and ability and not for any other reason. Elect people who are willing to serve, who are honest, and who have integrity.
3. Anybody who gives you money to solicit your vote is not confident and is showing what he will do in office. He or she is not fit for political office.
4. Elect a party that has a plan in place to fight corruption and that has a good plan (manifesto) for the country and the people.
5. Report anybody who is planning election irregularities such as rigging. Do not participate in such activities, whatever you are promised. You are harming yourself, your family, and your community if you do.
6. Your vote is your power to change. Use it wisely. Don't keep voting for the same corrupt politician who keeps putting themselves forward. Elect more honest politicians who have a good track record in ordinary lives. Elect people who go into politics to serve, not those whose aim is to get rich.
7. Keep an eye on the people that you employed to run your state. Express your views and preference through your representative.

8. The people that you elect are not a law on to themselves; they are accountable (report) to you, who elected them. They are not above the law.

9. Review their performance. Don't re-elect them if they do not keep their promise or if they are involved in corruption. (Nobody reemploys an employee that does not do his/her job well or who steals their property.)

10. Get involved. Fight corruption in politics/government for the sake of your state and for the future of your children and grandchildren.

11. Do not participate in or condone electoral fraud (vote rigging). The principle is one-man / one-vote to determine who has the greatest number of votes. Report electoral fraud. It is essential that election processes are fair; any political party that attempts to practice electoral fraud is not confident and is giving you a taste of its corrupt nature if it gets into power.

12. If you do not vote, you allow the few who vote to determine how the affairs of the country are run. The more people who vote, the better, as this will be more representative of the people's choice.

17

Corruption Eradication Statements.

1. Eradication of corruption starts with you.
2. Corruption is not a way of life. Break the cycle by eradicating it.
3. Change will not come on its own; it needs a direct and conscious effort on the part of the individual or group that requires the change.
4. Eradication of corruption starts with you. Yes, *you*. Those who are corrupt do not know any better—they are not honest; they are lazy and unwilling to work hard and do not want change.
5. Those who are honest are more than the corrupt; it not difficult to change the society if we make an effort.
6. Each citizen should determine to be anticorruption and expose corruption in their daily lives.
7. Teach children to value hard work and to be honest on all occasions. Teach love, compassion, and respect for their fellow human being. Respect for the laws of the country.
8. Do your work diligently and honestly as is in your job description.
9. There should be
   - Transparency and public openness to government activities.
   - A code of practice for top officials.
   - A good governance and reliability test in all institutions and public offices.

10. An independent media has a duty to expose corruption, not only reporting it but actively doing investigative journalism. It has a role in educating and championing the rights of the population.

11. The law-enforcement agencies and the judiciary should be purged of the corrupt elements. A well-trained and equipped police force and a merit appointed and a monitored judiciary is essential.

12. There must be education and overhaul of the people's perceptions and expectation about politics and politicians. This will result in the emergence of politicians who are patriotic, who have a vision, and who are in politics to serve and make a difference.

13. Rhetoric without action results in no movement. We must see politicians doing things to benefit the country.

14. Many multiracial, multi-tribal, and multi-religious nations run well and are prosperous because they think country—they are not patrician, tribal, or religion in their thinking and in action.

15. You cannot complain about or eradicate corruption if you keep electing the same corrupt politicians. Elect new politicians who have a vision for your country, not their own pockets. (Recycling old corrupt politicians is more fuel for more corruption.)

16. People should go into politics to serve, not to enrich themselves, to devote themselves selflessly to make their country great, peaceful, and prosperous.

17. Your vote is a precious commodity. You express your choice through your votes. Do not let the few who vote determine how your country is governed; be a part of the process. Remove corrupt politicians by not voting for them. Join a political party and influence decisions.

18. In a multi-tribal and multicultural country, the political appointments should reflect the various groups in the country. If this is not the case, there is bound to be a suspicion of an agenda to dominate if appointments favour a particular group or religion. No group should feel that they have a right to rule. There must be a common purpose to improve the lives of all the people, of all regions of the country. There should be freedom of speech and freedom to practice their religion.

19. True leaders use power to serve others and not to enrich themselves. The power and privileges that come with high office is to help you serve the people, not to oppress them.

20. Corruption results from leaders with a poor, poverty mentality. 'Woe to the land when a slave becomes king' —Solomon. A slave is stripped of everything and has a spirit of scarcity and lack and hence wants to acquire many things as quickly as possible. Corruption will be present when the leaders think like slaves. Greatness in leadership is in empowering others not pursuing power, serving others and not being served.

21. Corruption is a cancer that results from leaders who are selfish and who have low self-esteem, poor self-worth, fear of scarcity, and a high manifestation of insecurity.

22. Demand your rights; defend them and speak out if your rights or those of others are being infringed.

23. Depend on yourself abilities and talent. Do not depend on others to help you get you posts and jobs by influencing the process. This is corruption.

24. Nip corruption in the bud. Where it has grown to a tree, uproot it. Plant a seed of honesty in its place.

25. Most things in life are not instantaneous. There is no success without hard work. Things may be seasonal, and there are processes that take time to get result. The same is true of trying to eradicate corruption.

18

How to Start Making a Change

Making a lifelong change is a painful and difficult process which must start with the acceptance that something is not right and needs to change. It is a slow process, and people are often unwilling initially to change or move from their comfort zones but become proactive when a positive effect of the change is seen. Behavioural change involves time, effort, and emotion. It may involve small steps towards a bigger goal. Changes should be well managed, barriers to change must be identified, relapses are to be expected and must be managed, and there must be rewards, acknowledgement, support, and encouragement. It is important to maintain the change.

1. Change must starts with each individual who wishes to stand up against corrupt practices. Discuss corruption with your children and relatives. Teach by examples how to deal with its effect.
2. Form a group at work, in your club, among friends, in schools, and online. Know the people (local counsellors, members of state parliament/senate) that represent your area or region at local, regional, and at national levels. Know their constituency office and contact details. They represent you, and any issues that concern people in their constituency should be made known to them and should be discussed at the highest level. It is their job, and they must do it well.

3. Have a method of collecting opinions about issues that concerns everybody. Sign petitions in all walks of life and online (see organisations like www.change.org). Get the press and media involved. It is essential to have legislation in place for it to be mandatory for issues that the majority of the society is concerned about, to be discussed in parliament or the legislative assembly.

4. Lobby your representatives; involve the press, so that government will legislate to make it compulsory to get companies and government offices to have customer service and anticorruption policies. These must be functioning and monitored and must be available to the public. It must include training. Consequences of a breach must be serious. There should be a drive towards appointment to public office based on merit and experience and towards making holders of public office accountable for their actions and decisions.

5. Discuss current anticorruption laws and regulations and review them to see areas that the government needs to review, revise, and tighten. Lawyers in the group will help. Gets a campaign going to affect these changes.

6. Public funds. Review the current processes at all levels of government for disbursing public funds. Nobody should have the ability to take public money out for personal enrichment because of their official standing.

7. Contracts. Awarding process should be overhauled, preferably by an independent committee.

8. Law enforcement. An inefficient or absent law enforcement helps corruption to thrive. Corrupt people will get away with their crime if law enforcement is lacking or is corrupt. Individuals who are not corrupt do not want to get involved, if they know they have no protection from the law enforcement agencies and the judiciary.

9. The judiciary also needs an overhaul. Appointment and review of judges must be independent. The corrupt judges must be retired.

10. Code of conduct for public officials must be in place, reviewed, and enforced. Accountability of public officials to the people is essential for public confidence and assurance.

11. There should be a complete education of the population about politics. It is a job where the public elects a person/political party to serve the people and the country. It is not a job where you are elected to do nothing or to get rich by stealing or making laws to your own advantage or enrichment. Political parties should be more professional, have a vision for the whole country and not be partial as in some countries. Training and skill equipment of political aspirant should be a responsibility of the parties. Parties should be democratic and not controlled by a group/cartel in the party.

12. Government institutions and companies should by law have anticorruption policies. This policy should be displayed on site and available to the public. The policy should be monitored and reported annually. Good governance systems should be in place.

13. The ambiguity between appreciative giving and bribery should be clarified by a 'gift policy' document. Gifts should be discouraged and returned if inappropriate.

14. Education and literacy of the population and change of political attitudes is also an essential part of making a change.

19

Corruption Frequently Asked Questions

Q. What is Corruption?

A. Corruption means bribery, extortion, fraud, cartels, abuse of power, embezzlement, money-laundering, and other similar activities. Bribery appears to be the commonest form of corruption, but all are interlinked and the corrupt individual practices all in order to secure their office without being exposed. These activities benefit the individual at the expense of the community.

Q. Which are the most corrupt countries?

A. Corruption occurs in almost every country. It is more likely occur anywhere that there are no systems in place to prevent it and where the level of education population is poor, especially education about how the government runs. According to cnbc.com, published in January 2017, Somalia, South Sudan, North Korea, and Syria are perceived to be the most corrupt countries in the world, according to Transparency International's Ranking. They use the Corruption Perception Index 2016. A scale of 0–100 is used. The lower a country scores, the more corrupt it is. The countries perceived to be least corrupt are Denmark, New Zealand, and Finland.

Q. Why are there few attempts to fight corruption in some countries?

A. In a country where corruption is endemic and has become a way of life, everybody operates the system to get things done and to survive. Any non-corrupt voice or voices of dissent are suppressed by threats and violence, and there is no recourse to justice under the rule of law. To self-preserve, people are not incentivised to do anything. The corrupt government is unlikely to actively do something about corruption. It is usually a web that involves most of the top politicians, and it is self-destructive for any individual to attempt to do anything active about corruption.

Q. Does a people's culture contribute to propagation of corruption?
A. Corruption means doing the wrong things for the benefit of the corrupt at the expense of the community or individuals. All cultures appreciate honesty, order, and doing the right thing. Putting pressure on people in office to influence decision, using, religious, cultural, ethnic, or other factors is not right. There must be guidelines for decision making, and the official must be able to justify his/her decisions. In some 'generous' cultures, 'Giving' in appreciation may be used as an excuse for bribery. There are differences between the two. Bribery is demanded and given unlawfully to obtain services. Giving cements relationship; it is not demanded and demonstrates love and appreciation. A gift policy documents for industry and government institutions should clarify things.

Q. Some candidates' election expenses are sponsored by rich and powerful people/mentors. The sponsored candidate is expected to 'dance to the tune' of the sponsor when elected. How does one get around this?
A. The electoral commission's rules must be specific and sponsorship must be transparent. The individual sponsored must be honest and be determined not to be a puppet.

Q. How can we prevent the same corrupt politicians presenting themselves again for election?
A. This has to start with all of us who want change to become involved with the political system at the party level. The parties will be influenced to be transparent and to have policies that the people associate with and which will benefit the country. There should be training for the candidates and a transparent system of nominating candidates by the party members.

Young people should join the youth wing of their party and help to initiate change.

Q. How can other countries help to fight or eradicate corruption?
A. Other countries cannot interfere directly in the internal affairs of another country. Until the advent of money-laundering regulations, some countries benefitted from the monies that the corrupt politicians hid in their countries. Other countries can raise voices and through diplomatic sources, and the United Nations point out issues that affect human rights or that cause extreme suffering. Corrupt countries can be given incentives to fight and eradicate corruption.

Q. What can we do as a country to fight corruption?
A. The eradication of corruption starts with everybody who recognises the need for a change. Practice and teach your children the qualities of honesty, good character, integrity, hard work, and good work ethics. Teach them to love their country and preserve its unity, to respect the views and rights, and to have compassion on their fellow countrymen. Teach these qualities in schools and at all levels of education. Determine not give bribes and to expose and report corruption. Be a part of a group that advocate changes in your society. Elect the right people into office. Set up an anticorruption body (independent or government-led).

Q What is the corruption perception index?
A. This is a formula to assess the level of corruption in a country, and it serves as a comparative measure to determine the level of corruption between countries. Certain factors are used in this formula: literacy rate, expenditure on education (as a percentage of GDP), unemployment rate as a percentage of the population, the public-sector ethics index (0–100), the judicial/legal effectiveness index (0–100), the corporate governance index (0–100), and the Gini (statistical) index, which represents the wealth or income distribution of the nation's residents. It is a common measure of inequality. When computed, the formula CPI lies between 0 and 100, zero being the most corrupt and 100 the cleanest. To find your country's score, go to the website www.transparency.org/cpi2017.

Q What are the principles of good governance?
A. These include honesty, transparency, responsiveness, rule of law, effectiveness and efficiency, fairness, justice, accountability, and good management.

Q. What is gender egalitarianism in the community, and what is its effect on corruption?
A. This is an attempt to minimise the differences in roles of male and females in the home, organisation, and communities. Societies that do this have more women in positions of authority, and this has been shown to lower corruption levels.

Q. Am I corrupt if I gave a demanded bribe?
A. Corruption is both giving and receiving bribes, and both givers and receivers can be prosecuted under the law. It is best to decline, demand the regulation that states a fee is required for the service, and inform the demander/giver that you will report the incidence. You will find the GIACcentre.org recommendation useful at this link. http://www.giaccentre.org/individual_dealing_with_corruption.php

Q. How can I raise awareness and draw attention to issues resulting from corruption?
A. The anticorruption website Transparency.org offers the publication 'Anti-Corruption Kit: Fifteen Ideas for Young Activists' (https://www.transparency.org/whatwedo/publication/anti_corruption_kit_15_ideas_for_young_activists).

Q. How do I find out how corrupt my country is compared to the rest of the world?
A. The organisation Transparency publishes its Corruption Perception Index. This lists a table of corruption in countries. You will be able to see your country's ranking.

Q. In organisations, why do people who do not participate in corruption keep quiet and avoid speaking up about the corruption around them?
A. One of the reasons is a phenomenon called 'social proof'. This occurs in ambiguous or confusing situations. It is the tendency to take cues from

others in the vicinity on how to act (Cialdini 1993). People tend not to speak up or act in response to a stressful situation if they perceive that no one else witnessing that situation is speaking up or acting (Latané and Darley 1970). Any person can assume that others will do something about it. This leads to nothing being done about the issue. Other individuals in the group may think others' silence mean the situation is morally acceptable. These two effects may have a powerful influence on organisational members, who themselves neither receive nor make corrupt payments, to remain silent, even as others continue supporting the corrupt scheme.

20

Aids to Fight Corruption

Trying to reduce the level or eradicate corruption is a slow process and involves the individuals and the society collectively. The change has to be managed and relapses along the way tackled until improvements are sustained and become permanent. There may be initial apathy, but people are encouraged by the positive effects and benefits of the change.

Change may be government-led or by an organisation dedicated to fighting corruption. This must be a well-planned, dedicated, sustained, and prolonged campaign. The organisations must make it easy to report corruption and to persecute offenders. It must have an education arm for the population. These educational aids must be widely accessible through the various available media. The points below are some of the aids towards the fight.

1. Educating the people. In some countries, corruption has become such a way of life that people no longer think there are laws against corruption. Teaching of civics and ethics at all educational levels. Improvement in the literacy level in the population is a goal to be achieved. The family and homes is where foundations of good moral behaviour and character of an individual are laid.

2. Anticorruption policy in all government institutions and companies that are registered to operate in the country. This

should be monitored with yearly review and report. The policy should be widely available and accessible to the general population.

3. Good governance. The processes and the way a country is governed. There must be good governance processes in place. Reports (Harry Seldady and Jacob de Hann 2005) suggest that governance at a national level are full of bureaucracy and ineffectiveness, which affects the welfare of the people compared to governance at the sub-national level.

4. Making it easier to report or whistle blow on corruption. A dedicated government multidisciplinary body, which is made up of people who are honest and of proven integrity. They will look at and investigate reported cases.

    a. Forms and documents that make it easy to report cases should be easily accessible.

    b. Apps have been used in many countries to report corruption, upload documents/evidence, video, etc., from mobile phones and other devices. These will be reviewed and investigated by the appropriate bodies.

    c. Official government website. For information and education about corruption and how to report it in government institutions. This http://www.whistlenowkerala.com/ is worth looking at.

    d. Other resources that can be used include leaflets and publications and advertising campaigns.

    e. Podcasts and teaching materials van be downloaded from dedicated websites.

5. Reformation and efficiency of the law-enforcing agents and the judiciary. The law-abiding majority are frustrated because corrupt people are allowed to get away with it, either because of corruption or inefficiency of these crucial corruption-fighting and enforcing agencies.

6. Reversing the social factors that breed, encourage, and perpetuate corrupt practices.

    a. Improving the economy. Job creation, which reduces unemployment levels. Alleviation of the country's poverty level.

b. Regular payment of salaries and payment of government contractors.

c. Improvement of public facilities.

d. Respect for the rights and equal opportunities for all citizens, irrespective of their tribe, religion, or ethnicity.

e. Accessibility to justice. Improvement of the police and other law-enforcement agencies. Passing and implementation of anticorruption laws.

f. Improving the ethical standards of the public sector and society in general. Ethics is the moral principle which governs a person's behaviour or the performance of an activity. What was accepted years ago is no longer acceptable in the current age and needs to change. There is no growth if there is no change. A society that does not change is dead.

7. Resources available by international organisations that fight corruption.

a. Transparency International has publications that offer practical advice and describes projects and activities that can be used to educate and create anticorruption awareness.

b. Global Infrastructure Anticorruption Centre (GIACC) is an independent organisation which provides resources to assist in the understanding, identifying, and preventing corruption in the infrastructure, construction, and engineering sectors. It has sections on its website on how to deal with corruption by organisations, by the public, and by individuals. It also has anticorruption measures, programs, policies, and many more useful resources.

21

Further reading

The following is further reading, references, and links to articles/legislation and other relevant publications.

Corruption

1. 'Corruption and Development UND, A Primer', Dec 2008,www.undp.org/content/undp/en/home/librarypage/democratic-governance/anti-corruption/corruption.html.

2. Zawn Vlliness. Justifying Corruption
www.goodtherapy.org

3. Effects of Corruption. Its impact on people.
https://www.mindcontroversy.com/impact-effects-corruption-public-life/

4. 'The Determinants of Corruption: A Re-investigation', Henry Seldadyo and Jacob de Hann. 20 April 2006
https://projects.iq.harvard.edu/files/gov2126/files/seldadyo_determinants_corruption.pdf

5. Political,Social and Economic determinants of Corruption. Nafi Ghaniy et all 2017

http://dergipark.gov.tr/download/article-file/364553
http: www.econjournals.com

6. Police Corruption
Syed, T. 1997. 'Not Victimless: Understanding the Harmful Effects of Police Corruption', *Servamus* 91, no. 1.
https://www.csvr.org.za/publications/latest-publications/1485-not-victimless-understanding-the-harmful-effects-o

7. http://www.mindcontroversy.com/impact-effects-corruption-public-life-india/

8. www.corruptionwatch.org

9. CORRUPTION: AFRICA SURVEY 2015. GLOBAL CORRUPTION BAROMETER – Transparency International Publication.
www.afrobarometer.org

Teaching Anticorruption.

1. TRANSPARENCY INTERNATIONAL • 10 MARCH 2016 How to stop Coruption.
https://www.transparency.org/news/feature/how_to_stop_corruption_5_key_ingredients

2. *Teaching* Anticorruption. BOOK. www.ebooksdownloads.xyz/search/teaching-anticorruption

3. Anticorruption
https://en.wikipedia.org/wiki/Anti-corruption

4. Anticorruption Kit 15 Ideas for young Activists. Aug 11 2014
https://www.transparency.org/whatwedo/publication/anti_corruption_kit_15_ideas_for_young_activists

https://www.transparency.org/whatwedo/tools/anti_corruption_kit_15_ideas_for_young_activists/4

5. GIACC.Individuals Dealing with Corruption-Global infrastructure. May 1 2008
http://www.giaccentre.org/individual_dealing_with_corruption.php

Transparency.org

1. 'Awarding Contracts and Transparency', Transparency.org.

2. https://www.transparency.org/whatwedo/activity/curbing_corruption_in_public_procurement

3. http://www.open-contracting.org/get-started/global-principles/

4. https://www.transparency.org/whatwedo/publication/curbing_corruption_in_public_procurement_a_practical_guide

Culture and corruption

1. 'The Relationship between Culture and Corruption: A Cross-National Study', by Ahmed Seleim (Alexandria University, Alexandria, Egypt, and Beirut Arab University, Beirut, Lebanon) and Nick Bontis (DeGroote School of Business, McMaster University, Hamilton, Canada).
https://core.ac.uk/download/pdf/21748884.pdf

2. Adam Graycar & David Jancsics (2016): Gift Giving and Corruption, International Journal of Public Administration To link to this article:
http://dx.doi.org/10.1080/01900692.2016.1177833

3. Corporate Gifts. Acceptable practice vs Corruption. by Cynthia Schoeman. (Corruption Watch. December 2016)
https://www.corruptionwatch.org.za/corporate-gifts-acceptable-practice-vs-corruption/

https://www.corruptionwatch.org.za/corporate-gifts-

Governance

1. 'What Is Good Governance?' United Nations, ESCAP, https://www.unescap.org/sites/default/files/good-governance.pdf

2. 'Characteristics of Good Governance', www.gdrc.org.

Psychology of Corruption

1. Psychology of Corruption.—Giada Del Fabio et all. Corruption watch 25 June 2013
www.corruptionwatch.org.za/the-psychology-of-corruption/

2. 'Corruption: A Psychosocial Issue', Niranjan Prasad Upadhyay, https://www.repository.cam.ac.uk/bitstream/id/533648/OPSA_08_11.pdf/;jsessionid=EADED636DC0332DAA2505B0E8F63CF4A.

3. Occasional papers in *Sociology and Anthropology* 8 (2003)

4. 'Psycho-sociology of Corruption', Jonathan Rusch. http://www.oecd.org/cleangovbiz/Integrity-Forum-16-Jonathan-Rusch.pdf

5. www.psychologicalalliance.org For resources about cultural psychology. Human psychology.

6. Corruption, religion and Moral development
https://www.researchgate.net/publication/279667581_Corruption_religion_and_moral_development

Power and Corruption

1. Money, Politics, Power: Corruption Risks in Europe. Transparency.org report.
https://www.transparency.org/whatwedo/publication/money_politics_and_power_corruption_risks_in_europeJun 6, 2012

2. Transparency International is the global civil society organisation leading the fight against corruption. www.transparency.org
Other Reports by Transparency
issuu.com/transparencyinternational/docs/2014_anticorruptionkit_youth__en?e=2496456/8912943
https://issuu.com/transparencyinternational/docs/2014_anticorruption_publicprocureme

Money, Politics, Power and Corruption.

1. How likely are people to be corrupted by money. Business insider. June 2013
https://www.businessinsider.com/how-likely-people-are-to-be-corrupted-by-money-2013-6

2. "Seeing green: Mere exposure to money triggers a business decision frame and unethical outcomes" in the May 2013 issue of "Organizational Behavior and Human Decision Processes."

3. 'A Study of Party Financing Practices in 22 countries', edited by Shari Bryan and Denise Baer.

4. 'How power corrupts leaders' by Ronald E Riggio. in Psychology Today-August 8. 2009. https://www.psychologytoday.com/us/blog/cutting-edge-leadership/200908/how-power-corrupts-leaders